Orange **Line 4**

Vokabeltraining aktiv

Ernst Klett Verlag
Stuttgart • Leipzig

Hallo liebe Schülerin und lieber Schüler,

mit Vokabeltraining aktiv Orange Line 4 Grundkurs und Erweiterungskurs kannst du die wichtigsten neuen Vokabeln aus den Units noch einmal üben und wiederholen.

Wenn du mit dem **Grundkurs** lernst, dann bearbeite nur die Seiten mit den Übungen, die auf den **GK** verweisen. Wenn du mit dem **Erweiterungskurs** arbeitest, schaue nach den Seiten mit **EK**.

Es ist immer gut, neue Wörter in einem Satz zu lernen. Unter der Rubrik „What do you remember?“ gibt es auf der linken Seite jeweils deutsche Sätze mit blau unterstrichenen Lernwörtern aus deinem Englischbuch. Auf der rechten Seite findest du die entsprechenden englischen Sätze mit Lücken, die du am besten mit Bleistift ausfüllst.
Unten auf den Seiten findest du weitere Übungen, damit du die neuen Wörter noch einmal üben und ausprobieren kannst.

Hier ein Beispiel:

Der Oscar ist ein Preis für Schauspieler und sieht wie ein kleines Standbild aus. 	The Oscar is an ______________ for actors and looks like a small ______________ .	☐ ☐
Hast du Jesse Raymonds neues Album gehört? Er ist ein toller R&B Sänger.	Have you heard Jesse Raymond's new ______________? He's a great ______________ singer.	☐ ☐

Deine **Lösungen** kannst du auf den Seiten 71 – 79 selbst überprüfen. Achte dabei auf die korrekte Schreibung der Wörter. Hast du dich an die richtigen Wörter erinnert und sie fehlerfrei geschrieben, kannst du in die Kästchen am Rand ein Häkchen setzen.

Notiere die Wörter, bei denen du Schwierigkeiten hattest, und wiederhole sie. Du kannst z. B. Karteikarten mit den Wörtern anlegen und damit üben. Versuche dann erneut, die Lücken in den Sätzen zu vervollständigen.
Wenn du alle Wörter auf einer Seite „abgehakt“ hast, weißt du, dass du deine Vokabeln gut gelernt hast.

Viel Spaß und Erfolg mit deinem Vokabeltraining aktiv!

Tom

→ GK pages 8/9
→ EK pages 8/9

What do you remember?	
Was kannst du im Hintergrund des Bildes sehen?	What can you see in the ________________ of the picture?
Ich kann einen großen Wolkenkratzer sehen.	I can see a tall ____________________.
Im Vordergrund des Bildes ist die Freiheitsstatue.	In the ____________________ of the picture is the Statue of Liberty.
Diese Statue ist ein Symbol für die Freiheit.	This statue is a ______________ of ______________.
Du kannst die Freiheitsstatue besteigen – aber es sind 354 Stufen!	You can climb the Statue of Liberty – but there are 354 ________!
Am Hafen läuft ein Jogger sehr schnell.	At the ____________ a ____________ is running very quickly.
Die meisten Wolkenkratzer sind im Bezirk Manhattan.	Most skyscrapers are in the ____________ of Manhattan.
Anna spielt mit ihrem Roller im Central Park.	Anna is playing with her ______________ in Central Park.
Central Park ist der größte öffentliche Park.	Central Park is the biggest ____________ park.
Die ersten Einwanderer wohnten in den ärmsten Vierteln.	The first ________________ lived in the poorest ____________________.
Vor dem Theater kannst du ein großes neonfarbenes Schild sehen.	In front of the ____________ you can see a big ____________ sign.

1 Definition

Tick the right definition for each word.

1. theater
   - ☐ a. People run there.
   - ☐ b. a part of town
   - ☐ c. You can watch shows there.
2. borough
   - ☐ a. one of the five areas in New York
   - ☐ b. a kind of boat
   - ☐ c. part of a kickboard
3. jogger
   - ☐ a. a person on a kickboard
   - ☐ b. a runner
   - ☐ c. a person from Brooklyn
4. public
   - ☐ a. not private
   - ☐ b. not expensive
   - ☐ c. not far
5. harbor
   - ☐ a. You can sit on the grass there.
   - ☐ b. You can see many ships there.
   - ☐ c. You can buy CDs there.
6. skyscraper
   - ☐ a. a small plane
   - ☐ b. a kind of school
   - ☐ c. a very tall building

→ GK page 10
→ EK page 10

What do you remember?	
Einwanderung ist immer noch ein Thema in den Nachrichten.	______ is still a topic in the news.
Viele Einwanderer fliehen vor einem Krieg in ihrem Heimatland.	Many immigrants escape from a ______ in their home country.
Die Niederländer gründeten New Amsterdam 1626.	The ______ ______ New Amsterdam in 1626.
Die Engländer nannten die Stadt später New York.	The ______ later ______ the city New York.
Die Iren kamen in großen Schiffen.	The ______ came in big ships.
In einer Hungersnot haben die Menschen nichts zu essen.	In a ______ people don't have anything to eat.
1921 brauchten die USA eine Einwanderungsquote.	In 1921 the USA needed an immigration ______.

2 Find the mistakes

Find the mistakes and correct the words.

1. There was a femine in Ireland. ______
2. Many of the Irelanders landed at Castle Garden. ______
3. The Deutsch founded New Amsterdam. ______
4. The Statue of Liberty is a symbol of freadom. ______
5. There are high levels of immigration during wors. ______
6. Immigration quotes are sometimes very strict. ______
7. Were the Dutch or the Englisch there first? ______
8. What will she names her baby? ______
9. Is imigration a problem or a good thing? ______
10. I think it's the tallest skyscrapper in the USA. ______
11. Which burough do you live in? ______
12. The boy is sitting on the stepps. ______

→ GK pages 10/11
→ EK page 10

What do you remember?		
Viele Leute auf den Schiffen waren seekrank.	Many people on the ships were ______________.	☐
Ein Beamter stellte den Leuten viele Fragen.	An ______________ asked the people many questions.	☐
Brüssel ist eine berühmte belgische Stadt.	Brussels is a famous ______________ city.	☐
Wenn die Zeit abgelaufen ist, beenden die Spieler das Spiel.	When the time has ______________, the players finish the game.	☐
Die meisten Leute sind aufgeregt, wenn sie auswandern.	Most people feel excited when they ______________.	☐
Heute leben einige Ureinwohner Amerikas in Armut.	Today some ____________ ______________ live in ______________.	☐ ☐
Sie wurde in Brüssel geboren, also ist sie gebürtige Belgierin.	She was born in Brussels, so she is a __________ Belgian.	☐
Unterdrückung ist nicht gerecht und sollte nicht geschehen.	______________ isn't fair and shouldn't happen.	☐

3 Questions and answers

Match the questions with the correct answers.

1. Do you feel seasick?
2. Has the Belgian quota already run out?
3. Who lived on Little Oyster Island first?
4. Are the immigrants escaping oppression?
5. Which city did the English name New York?

a. The native Americans were there before the Dutch.
b. No, they're escaping poverty.
c. Yes, and I was only at the harbor!
d. I think that was New Amsterdam.
e. Yes. That means you must go home.

4 Letter puzzle

Put the German words into English and write them in the correct place.

1. Belgierin
2. auswandern
3. Beamtin
4. seekrank
5. eingeboren
6. Engländer

1						☐	F	☐	☐	☐	☐	☐	☐
2						☐	A	☐	☐	☐	☐		
3						☐	M	☐	☐	☐	☐	☐	☐
4			☐	☐	☐	☐	I	☐	☐				
5	☐	☐	☐	☐	☐	☐	N						
6						☐	E	☐	☐	☐	☐	☐	

→ EK pages 8/12

What do you remember?	
Das Lieblingsspielzeug meiner Katze ist ein Knäuel Garn.	My cat's favourite toy is a ______ of ______.
Wenn es sich abwickelt, spielt sie stundenlang damit.	When it ______, she plays with it for hours.
Sie läuft zu dem Zwirn und springt darauf. Echt süß!	She runs to the ______ and jumps on it. Really sweet!
New York ist ein Zentrum für neue Mode.	New York is a ______ for new fashion.
Als das Auto immer weiter weg fuhr, winkten wir alle.	As the car drove ______ away, we all waved.
„Hast du noch Hoffnung, dass du den Times Square finden kannst?"	"Have you still got ______ that you can find Times Square?"
„Nur wenig! Ich glaube, wir sind weiter weg als vorher!"	"Only a ______! I think we are ______ away than before!"
„Lasst uns an dieser Imbissstube anhalten. Wir könnten einen Kaffee trinken und den Stadtplan ansehen."	"Let's stop at this deli. We could have a ______ and look at the map."
„Meiner Meinung nach ist das die beste Idee, die ich heute gehört habe!"	"In my ______ that's the best idea which I've heard today!"

5 Phonetics

Read the words. Then write them down correctly.

1. ['kɒfiː] ______
2. ['lɪtl] ______
3. [hʌb] ______
4. [həʊp] ______
5. [bɔːl] ______
6. [θred] ______
7. [ə'pɪnjən] ______
8. [ʌn'waɪnd] ______
9. [ʌn'waʊnd] ______
10. [jɑːn] ______
11. ['fɑːðə] ______
12. ['siːsɪk] ______

6 More letters than you need

You only need every second letter. The words are from the grid above.

1. jyealrmn ______
2. puanrwfivnsd ______
3. sheorpie ______
4. gfzayrhtthoemr ______
5. cheulb ______
6. kcaorfvfiece ______
7. ftkhsrqecajd ______
8. plriytwtilie ______

→ GK pages 12/13
→ EK pages 12/13

What do you remember?	
Anna und Tim sind in New York im Urlaub.	Anna and Tim are on ________________ in New York.
Sie sind zum Mittagessen in eine Imbissstube gegangen.	They have gone to a ______________ for lunch.
„Die Bagels sehen gut aus, aber acht Dollar ist teuer“, sagt Tim.	“The ______________ look good, but eight ______________ is expensive,” says Tim.
„Aber sie sind eine Spezialität in New York, deshalb kaufe ich dir einen“, sagt Anna.	“But they are a ______________ in New York, so I will buy you one,” says Anna.
„Toll! Ich möchte einen Bagel mit Frischkäse und ein Kirsch-Eis.“	“Great! I would like a bagel with ____________________ and a ________________ ice-cream.”
Anna nimmt Pommes frites und ein Stück Erdbeerkuchen.	Anna has ________________________ and a piece of ____________________ cake.
Aber sie hat nicht genug Geld. „Hast du fünf Cent, Tim?“	But she doesn’t have enough money. “Have you got five ____________ Tim?”
Tim gibt Anna einen Nickel.	Tim gives Anna a _______________.
Dann isst er seinen Bagel sehr schnell. „Du bist ein Monster!“ schreit Anna.	Then he eats his bagel very quickly. “You’re a ______________!” shouts Anna.
Als Trinkgeld legt Anna drei Vierteldollar auf den Tisch.	For a ______ Anna puts three ____________ on the table.
„Danke“, sagt der Mann. Er gibt Anna ein rundes Küchlein und das ist natürlich kostenlos.	“Thanks,” says the man. He gives Anna a _______________ and that is _____________, of course.

7 Which word is it?

Choose the right word from the grid above and complete the definitions.

1. A scary animal in fiction is a ____________________.
2. There are 100 cents in a ____________________.
3. A ____________________ is a small, dark red fruit.
4. You don‘t have to work or study when you‘re on ____________________.
5. 25 cents are also called a ____________________ and 5 cents are also called a ____________________.
6. ____________________ are a potato snack that you often eat with a burger.
7. When you don‘t have to pay for something, it‘s ____________________.

→ GK pages 12/13
→ EK pages 12/13

What do you remember?

Viele Leute essen ein Plundergebäck zum Frühstück.	Many people eat a ______________ for breakfast.	☐
Man kann sie auch zum Mitnehmen kaufen.	You can also buy them ______________ .	☐
Aber ich finde, Toast schmeckt besser. Am Wochenende mache ich Pfannkuchen.	But I think ______________ is tastier. On weekends I make ______________ .	☐ ☐
Sie schmecken gut mit Ahornsirup.	They taste good with ______________ .	☐
Aber am besten schmecken sie mit viel Sahne.	But they taste best with lots of ______________ .	☐
Zum Mittagessen mag ich einen Bagel mit Schinkenspeck.	For lunch I like a bagel with ______________ .	☐
Oft bestelle ich meinen Bagel mit einer Scheibe Tomate.	I often order my bagel with a ______________ of tomato.	☐
Könnten Sie bitte mehr Tomate hinzufügen?	Could you ______________ more tomatoes, please?	☐
Ja, aber das kostet noch ein Zehncentstück, bitte.	Yes, but that's another ______________ , please.	☐
Und dazu hätte ich gerne einen Milchshake.	And I would like a ______________ with it.	☐
Ich hasse Truthahn und Pastrami! Die schmecken beide furchtbar.	I hate ______________ and ______________ ! They both taste horrible.	☐ ☐

8 Word search

Look for ten kinds of food.
You find them across → and down ↓.

T	R	B	A	C	O	N	O	O	B	D	X
O	A	S	P	V	B	Z	X	R	A	I	I
D	A	N	T	F	L	T	E	A	G	N	O
C	U	P	C	A	K	E	A	C	E	P	T
C	R	A	Y	P	E	S	Y	R	L	A	E
W	C	R	E	A	M	C	H	E	E	S	E
E	L	I	S	N	H	A	Y	A	B	T	Z
S	L	T	E	C	T	A	P	M	V	R	Q
F	A	S	G	A	O	T	B	N	O	A	O
M	A	T	R	K	A	T	O	A	S	M	B
M	A	P	L	E	S	Y	R	U	P	I	U
V	E	R	R	E	T	U	R	K	E	Y	Y

→ GK page 14
→ EK page 14

What do you remember?		
Hast du das Fest und den tollen Umzug genossen?	Did you enjoy the ________ and the brilliant ________?	☐ ☐
Einige Läden und Geschäfte sind bis 22 Uhr geöffnet.	Some shops and ________ are open until 10 p.m.	☐
Hast du schon die schönen Dekorationen im Fenster dieses kleinen Ladens gesehen?	Have you already looked at the beautiful ________ in the window of that little shop?	☐
Um wie viel Uhr fängt das Feuerwerk an?	What time do the ________ start?	☐
Um 20 Uhr. Es wird eine halbe Stunde andauern.	At 8 p.m. They will ________ for half an hour.	☐
Der Mann, der uns geholfen hat, war sehr freundlich.	That man who helped us was very ________.	☐
Was für ein großer roter Drache! Könntest du so einen aus Papier machen?	What a big red ________! Could you make one like that out of ________?	☐ ☐

9 Festival time

Put in the right words.

business • decorations • festival • fireworks • friendly • goes on • paper • parade • vacation

"The ________ starts on Friday and even the weather should be good," said Emma.

"Yes," said Carrie. "I'm very excited and I really love the loud ________."

"Really?" asks Emma. "My favourite part is the ________ in the street. It ________ for two hours! And the people are really ________."

"Yes," said Carrie. "You're right. I missed it last year because I was on ________ in Canada."

"Maybe we should make some ________," said Emma. "But first we need to buy some ________."

"No, we don't."

"Why not?"

"Because my dad has a paper ________. I get all my paper for free!"

→ EK page 14

What do you remember?		
Deutschland hat eine größere Bevölkerung als Großbritannien.	Germany has a bigger ______________ than Great Britain.	☐
Kinder bekommen oft Süßigkeiten wie Schokolade zum Geburtstag.	Children often get ______________, ______________ chocolate, on their birthday.	☐☐
Unter dem Fenster steht ein niedriger Tisch.	There is a ______________ table under the window.	☐
Viele Leute genießen aufregende Aktivitäten.	Lots of people enjoy exciting ______________.	☐
Die Filme, die mir gefallen, sind größtenteils lustig, aber ich schaue auch Dokumentarfilme an.	The films which I like are ______________ funny but I watch documentaries, too.	☐
Die unteren Teile des Gebäudes sind Geschäfte. Oberhalb der Geschäfte wohnen Leute.	The ______________ parts of the building are shops. People live above the shops.	☐

10 Missing letters

Add the missing letters and complete the words from the grid above.

1. _ c _ i _ _ _ _ _ _
2. _ _ w
3. _ _ s _ _ y
4. _ a _ _ _
5. s _ _ _ _ s
6. _ _ _ e _
7. _ o _ _ _ _ _ _ o _

11 Odd man out

Which word doesn't fit? Underline it.

1. low – high – under – large
2. teacher – population – nurse – pupil
3. biggest – higher – lower – more friendly
4. cat – dog – horse – dragon
5. New York – London – Ireland – Paris
6. dime – pound – nickel – quarter
7. candy – coffee – bagel – cherry
8. paper – bed – wood – glass

→ GK page 16
→ EK page 16

What do you remember?	
Gestern schauten wir uns Flugzeuge an. Sie waren sehr laut und dröhnten.	Yesterday we watched planes. They were very loud and ______.
Wir standen auf einem flachen Dach am Flughafen.	We stood on a ______ roof at the airport.
„Um wie viel Uhr hebt das Flugzeug ab?“	“What time does the plane ______?”
„Um 16 Uhr, glaube ich. Ich möchte unbedingt einen Schnappschuss machen!“	“At 4 p.m., I think. I really want to take a ______!”
Als ich das Foto machte, blitzte meine Kamera. Der Pilot sah mich und winkte.	When I took the photo, my camera ______. The ______ saw me and waved.
„Habt ihr eine Stadtrundfahrt gemacht, als ihr in New York wart?“	“Did you do a city ______ when you were in New York?”
„Ja, natürlich! Das war unser allererster Urlaub dort.“	“______, of course! That was our ______ first vacation there.”
Wir waren in einem Bus, also konnten wir uns einfach zurücklehnen.	We were in a bus, so we could just ______.
Innen im Bus war es echt kühl.	Inside the bus it was really ______.
Als wir am Empire State Building vorbeifuhren, deutete Tim darauf und sagte: „Schaut euch das an, Leute!”	When we drove past the Empire State Building, Tim ______ it and said, “Look at that, ______!”

12 What kind of word?

Put the words from the grid into the correct column. Find at least two words for each column.

Verb	Noun

Adjective	Other

→ GK pages 16/17
→ EK pages 16/17

What do you remember?	
Gestern betrug die Temperatur in New York 104° Fahrenheit – was für eine Hitze!	Yesterday the temperature in New York was 104° ______________ – what a __________!
Ich wurde ohnmächtig, als ich im Zug war.	I ______________ when I was on the train.
Mein Freund fand einen Polizisten, der mir Wasser gab.	My friend found a __________ who gave me some water.
Wenn ich jetzt in der Stadt herum laufe, habe ich immer Wasser bei mir!	Now when I walk ______________ the city, I always have water with me!
Diese Sendung ist langweilig. Lasst uns den Fernseher ausschalten!	This show is boring. Let's ______________ the TV!
Anna war nach dem schnellen Tanz schwindelig.	Anna was ___________ after the fast dance.
Ich habe gerade eine neue elektrische Türklingel gekauft.	I've just bought a new _____________ doorbell.
Oh nein, die Tür ist schon wieder kaputt! Wir müssen den Handwerker anrufen.	Oh no, the door is broken again! We need to call the ______________ .
Lass mich meine Bohrmaschine holen und dann schauen wir, ob ich sie reparieren kann.	Let me get my ____________ and then let's see if I can ______________ it.
„Entschuldigen Sie, wissen Sie wann die Aufführung heute Abend beginnt?"	"Excuse me, ________________ , do you know what time the performance begins this evening?"

13 Which word is it?

Choose the right word and complete the sentences.

1. I saw a ______________ on 42nd Street.

2. It was so sunny that I fainted in the ____________.

3. Forty degrees Celsius is 104 degrees _____________________.

4. My bed was broken so I asked a _____________________ to _________________ it.

→ EK pages 16/17

What do you remember?	
Es ist immer wichtig, Anweisungen zu befolgen.	It is always important to follow ______________.
Ich kann ziemlich gut kochen, aber nicht so gut wie mein Vater.	I can cook ______________ well, but not as well as my father.
An welchen Hobbies bist du interessiert?	Which hobbies ______________ you ______________?
Während ich mich an dich lehnte, war ich sehr schläfrig.	While I ______________ on you, I was very sleepy.
In meiner neuen Wohnung kann ich mich sehr gut entspannen.	In my new ______________ I can ______________ very well.
Lehn dich nicht so sehr nach vorne, sonst fällst du vom Dach herunter!	Don't lean ______________ that much or you'll fall off the roof!
Welche Art von Geschäften gibt es auf der 5th Avenue?	What ______________ of shops are there on 5th Avenue?
Ich sammle CDs, also habe ich viele davon – ungefähr 250!	I collect CDs, so I've got ______________ them – about 250!

14 Rhyming words

Find rhyming pairs.

quite • relax • lean • sort • loads

1. roads ______________
2. screen ______________
3. light ______________
4. snacks ______________
5. caught ______________

15 The same

Add a word with the same meaning from the grid above.

1. kind = ______________
2. flat = ______________
3. to be interested in = ______________
4. many = ______________

16 Teacher talk

What is the teacher saying? Write it down.

____

____

____

[liːn ˈfɔːwəd ænd ˈlɪsn tə maɪ ɪnˈstrʌkʃns! wiː həv gɒt ləʊdz‿əv wɜːk tə duː!]

→ GK pages 8/18

What do you remember?	
Hast du den ganzen Kuchen alleine gegessen? Das ist verrückt!	Did you eat the ____________ cake alone? That's crazy!
Wir sollten bald nach Hause gehen. Es ist schon ziemlich spät.	We should go home soon. It's already ____________ late.
Ich glaube, dass der Motor eines Flugzeugs etwa 200 Prozent lauter ist als der eines Autos.	I think that a plane's ____________ is about 200 ____________ louder than a car's.
Was für ein altes Haus! Ich kann sogar Mäuse unterhalb des Fußbodens hören.	What an old house! I can even hear mice ____________ the floor.
Bitte markiere die Straße unseres Hotels auf dem Stadtplan.	Please ____________ the street of our hotel on the map.
Die Menschen, die einwanderten, kamen von überall auf der Welt.	The people who ____________ came from ____________ the world.
Als ich meinen Lieblingsfußballer sah, wollte ich zu ihm hinüberrennen, aber ich kam nicht durch die riesige Menschenmenge.	When I saw my favourite football player, I wanted to ____________ to him, but I couldn't get through the ____________ crowd.
Im oberen Teil des Empire State Building gibt es ein Café.	At the ____________ of the Empire State Building there is a café.
Der Anfang des Buches war ein bisschen langweilig, aber dann wurde es echt spannend.	The ____________ of the book was a bit boring, but then it became really exciting.
Hast du den Fahrer im vorderen Teil des Zuges gesehen?	Did you see the driver ____________ of the train?

17 What can you say?

Match the two parts of the sentences.

1. Fourteen per cent of the population of the United Kingdom
2. A huge number of Americans
3. There was a pretty big dragon
4. I was at the top
5. A picture of an engine
6. The whole festival
7. My friend said there were cops all over

a. and I saw my brother below.
b. is about new beginnings.
c. were born outside the USA.
d. because there was an emergency.
e. live in London.
f. is at the front of my science book.
g. at the parade.

Revision

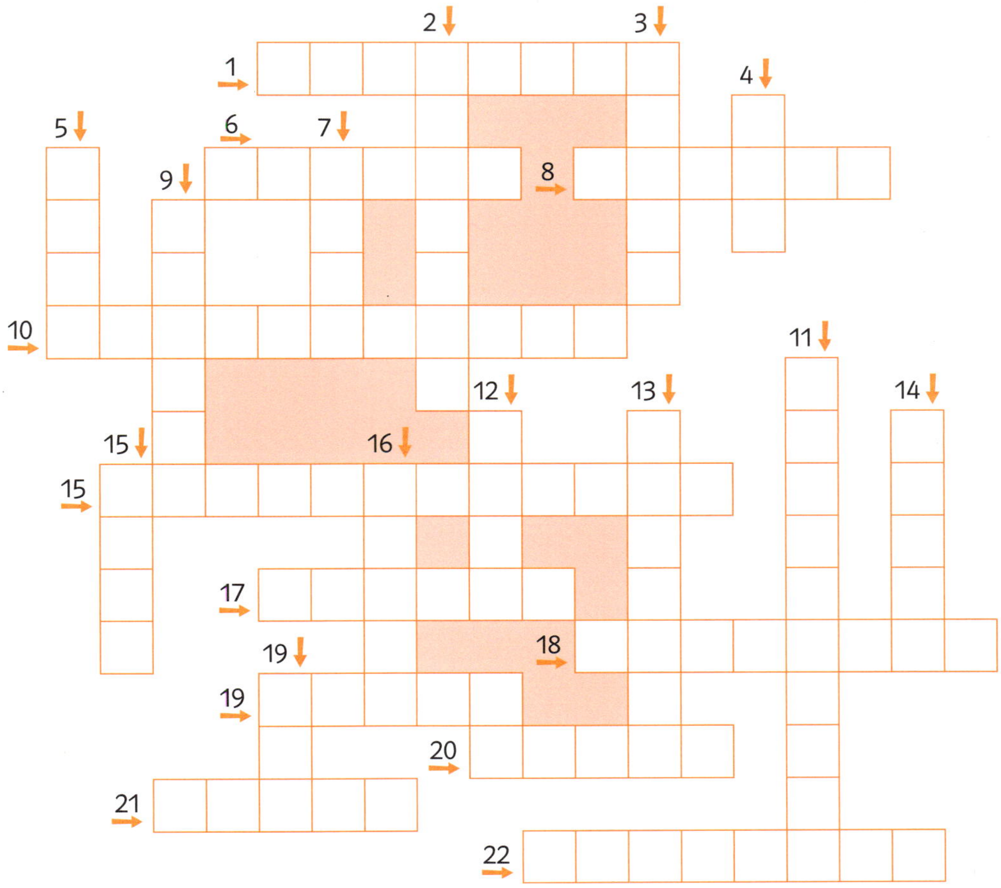

Across

1. another word for photo
6. … Americans lived in America before the Dutch arrived.
8. The … moved along the street at the festival.
10. People arrive in a new country to live there.
15. All the houses and streets around your house are your …
17. five cents
18. to leave a country and go and live in a new one
19. There are 100 … in a dollar.
20. Some people … when it is too hot or when they are shocked.
21. 
22. She welcomed me. She was very nice and …

Down

2. People don't have much money here. They live in …
3. hot bread for breakfast
4. The two countries are fighting. They are at …
5. You can buy breakfast, coffee and sandwiches here.
7. a trip from one place to another
9. If there is no food in a country, there is a …
11. The people are in the foreground and the city is in the … of the picture.
12. I didn't take any money because the festival was …
13. This person works with his hands and repairs things.
14. 
15. Times Square is full of … lights.
16. This meat comes from pigs and is popular at breakfast time in America.
19. policeman

→ GK page 22
→ EK page 24

What do you remember?

Anna hat einen Preis für ihr Geschichtsprojekt gewonnen. Ich glaube, dass sie die beste Schülerin der Schule ist.	Anna has won a __________ for her History project. I think that she is the school's best __________.
Du kannst den Lehrplan der Schule auf der Website lesen.	You can read the school's __________ on the website.
Wirst du deine High School vermissen, wenn du sie verlassen hast?	Will you miss your __________ when you have left?
Gibt es bei der Schulversammlung auch Musik?	Will there be music, too, at the school __________?
Die Cheerleader üben für das Homecoming im September dieses Jahres.	The __________ are practising for this year's __________ in September.
Zuerst musst du zum Auswahlverfahren gehen. Jede Schülerin von Klasse 8 bis 10 kann daran teilnehmen.	First you must go to a __________. Every student from 8th to 10th __________ can take part in it.
Hast du die neuesten Nachrichten gehört? Bald wird hier ein neuer Freizeitpark aufmachen!	Have you heard the __________? Soon a new __________ will open here!
Das ist ein tolles Foto für unser Jahrbuch!	This is a great photo for our __________!

1 Mrs O'Brien's school days

Put in the right words.

breaking news • cheerleaders • curriculum • grade • high school • homecoming • prizes • student • tryouts • yearbook

"When I started __________, everything was very different," said Mrs O'Brien. "We didn't have a __________ with a photo of every __________ in the school. And we didn't have __________ at football games."

"So no __________ to find the best cheerleaders! Did you have __________ for the best students?" asked Jim.

"Yes, that started when I was in 10th __________. School subjects were different, too."

"I understand. So it wasn't the same __________. Did you have __________ at the start of the year?"

"Oh, yes! Homecoming isn't __________! It's an old tradition."

→ GK page 23
→ EK page 25

What do you remember?		
Wenn du etwas gelobst, versprichst du es.	When you ____________ something, you promise it.	☐
Mein Lieblingshobby ist Gesellschaftstanz, obwohl es nicht jeder mag.	____________ is my favourite hobby although not ____________ likes it.	☐ ☐
Hast du die Ballkönigin gesehen? Sie trägt ein schönes blaues Kleid.	Have you seen the ____________? She's wearing a beautiful blue ____________.	☐ ☐
Der Kapitän der Fußballmannschaft dankte seinen Anhängern.	The ____________ of the football team thanked his ____________.	☐ ☐
Du kannst zu Bobs Feier keine Jeans tragen – wenigstens nicht während des formellen Teils!	You can't wear ____________ to Bob's party – at least not during the ____________ part!	☐ ☐
Beim Jugendtreffen gefielen mir das Tanzen und die Pompons der Cheerleader am besten.	At the rally I liked the ____________ and the ____________ of the cheerleaders best.	☐ ☐
Die Klasse baute Dekorationen aus Papier im Ballsaal auf.	The class put up paper decorations in the ____________.	☐
Nach dem Siegtreffer sangen die Fans wie verrückt.	After the winning goal the fans ____________ like mad.	☐
Hast du Emmas Auto gesehen? Es ist brandneu.	Have you seen Emma's car? It's ____________ new.	☐
Die Schüler müssen der Flagge und ihrem Land die Treue geloben.	The students must pledge ____________ to the flag and to their country.	☐

2 More letters than you need

You only need every third letter. The words are from the grid above.

1. zpfbaobdrinmceapyl ____________
2. hsckshiuarknckt ____________
3. topolondmmlpiuofxm ____________
4. deartlnmlghedfgcvioiamjnsscqae ____________

3 The correct word

Complete the sentences and underline the correct word.

1. This year Emily will be the homecoming *(girl/queen/sister)*.
2. Another word for 'fan' is *(supporter/player/rally)*.
3. Every morning the pupils pledge *(dress/allegiance/curriculum)* to the American flag.
4. *(Skirts/Shoes/Jeans)* are trousers but they aren't formal!
5. The *(captain/cheerleader/supporter)* of the football team chooses the players.

→ GK pages 24/25
→ EK pages 26/27

What do you remember?

Während Taras Abwesenheit setzte sich ihre Lehrerin mit Taras Eltern in Verbindung.	During Tara's ______________ her teacher ______________ Tara's parents.
Hast du gehört? Helens Eltern haben Alkohol in ihrem Schlafzimmer gefunden. Glücklicherweise war ich seit Langem nicht mehr dort!	Did you hear? Helen's parents found ______________ in her bedroom. ______________ I haven't been there for a long time!
Für den Schulausflug brauchst du die Erlaubnis deiner Eltern. Bring diesen Schein wieder mit in die Schule.	You need your parents' ______________ for the school trip. Bring this ______________ back to school.
Letzte Woche habe ich mich mit Matthew verabredet.	Last week I ______________ Matthew.
In Großbritannien sieht man nicht so viele Anzeigen für Tabak.	In Great Britain you don't see so many ______________ for ______________.
In den USA bekommt man vom Arzt Medikamente, wenn man krank ist.	In the US you get ______________ from the doctor when you are sick.
Hast du genügend Stoff für dein Kunstprojekt gesammelt?	Have you collected enough ______________ for your Art project?
Banden sind manchmal ein echtes Problem in Schulen.	______________ are sometimes a real problem in schools.

4 Crossword

Read the clues and then complete the crossword.

Across →

1. I need to … Lisa. I'll phone or text her.
4. He really likes Sarah and he would love to … her.
5. In the US you mustn't drink … if you're under 21.
7. Children need … to leave the table.

Down ↓

2. Many people smoke but … is a dangerous drug.
3. It was a very bad accident, but … the driver didn't die.
5. I saw an … for that car in a magazine.
6. Dad, please sign this … for me.

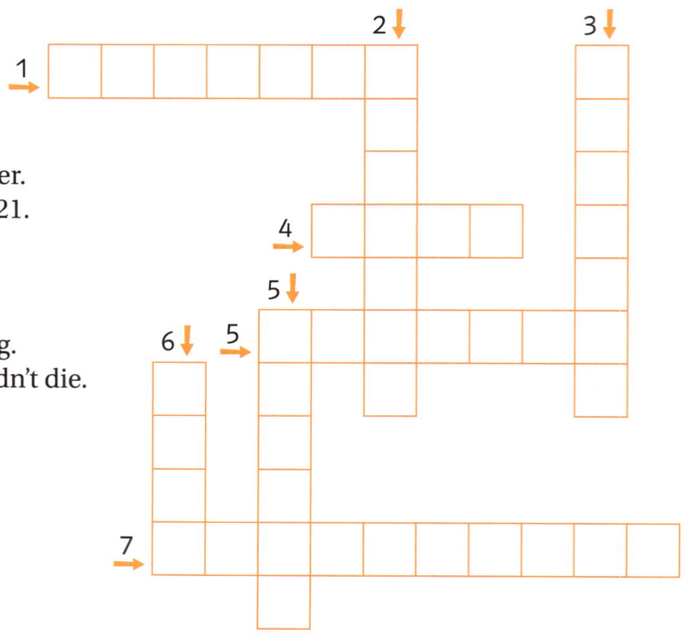

→ EK pages 24/27

What do you remember?		
Es gibt immer eine Pause nach der vierten Unterrichtsstunde.	We always have ______ after fourth ______.	☐ ☐
Wem gehört diese Tasche? Ich habe sie nie zuvor gesehen. Bitte wirf einen Blick auf sie.	Who does this bag ______? I've never seen it before. Please ______ it.	☐ ☐
Hast du diese coole Bildunterschrift gesehen? Ich wünsche, ich könnte mir solche Sachen ausdenken!	Have you seen this cool ______? I wish I could ______ things like that!	☐ ☐
Erwachsene sind mindestens 21 Jahre alt.	______ are at least 21 years old.	☐
Wenn man einen Text bearbeitet, sucht man darin die Fehler.	When you ______ a text, you look for the mistakes in it.	☐
Am Flughafen ging meine Mutter direkt zur Raucherzone.	At the airport my mother went ______ to the smoking ______.	☐ ☐
Es gibt einen großen Unterschied zwischen einem Film auf DVD und im Kino.	There is a big ______ between a film on DVD and in the cinema.	☐
Mindestens ein Elternteil muss dein Zeugnis unterschreiben!	At least one ______ must sign your ______!	☐ ☐
Darf ich bitte Ihren Reisepass sehen?	______ I see your passport, please?	☐
Warum warst du bei unserer Schwimmstunde abwesend?	Why were you ______ from our swimming lesson?	☐

5 What can you say?

Match the two parts of the sentences.

1. You need permission from a parent
2. He said he had edited the letter
3. After recess
4. I must go straight home
5. She had a look at the photo
6. You may not smoke
7. This prize belongs to Daniel
8. When our teacher found the drugs,

a. but when I read it, I didn't see any difference.
b. he contacted all the parents immediately.
c. but he is absent today.
d. or another adult.
e. in the tobacco-free zone.
f. it's the third period.
g. and thought up a great caption.
h. after I've written this report.

→ GK pages 26/27
→ EK pages 28/29

What do you remember?	
Letzten Samstag hatte ich eine tolle Verabredung mit einem sehr attraktiven Mädchen.	Last Saturday I went on a great ____________ with a very ____________ girl.
Wir haben den Film „Der Zoowärter" gesehen. Er war für Kinder, aber er hat mir dennoch gefallen.	We saw the ____________ *The Zookeeper*. It was for children, but I ____________ liked it.
Wir haben uns um 19 Uhr vor dem Kino getroffen und sie sagte einfach „Hallo!"	We met in front of the ____________ at 7 p.m. and she just said, "____________!".
Ich wollte es nicht übertreiben, aber ich brachte ihr ein kleines Geschenk mit. Ich wollte aufmerksam sein.	I didn't want to ____________ it, but I brought her a small present. I wanted to be ____________.
Als es Zeit war, den Abend zu beenden und nach Hause zu gehen, versuchte ich ihr einen Kuss zu geben.	When it was time to ____________ the evening and go home, I tried to give her a ____________.
Ich machte eine Bewegung auf sie zu, aber sie drehte sich um und sagte: „Bis dann!"	I made a ____________ towards her but she turned and said, "____________!"
Doch dann bekam ich eine SMS von ihr. Sie lautete: „Ich dachte, du bist ein Trottel, aber ich hatte Unrecht. Wie wäre es mit einer echt scharfen Verabredung nächste Woche?"	But then I got a text message from her. It said, "I thought you were a ____________ but I was wrong. What about a really ____________ date next week?"
Hey, ist das nicht toll?!!	Hey, isn't that ____________?!!

6 Find the mistakes

Find two words in each sentence that are not correct. Then write them correctly on the lines.

1. "Hi, their!" he shouted. "Did you go to the tryaut?" ____________ ____________
2. "This rallie was fantastic! So, sea you around!" ____________ ____________
3. The jurk was smoking tobbaco at school. ____________ ____________
4. The movie wasn't awesum but I stell had fun. ____________ ____________
5. I had a deight with Kelly at the moovies last night. ____________ ____________
6. Tell her she is attraktive but don't overdoe it. ____________ ____________
7. It was a really whot date, but he didn't make a muve. ____________ ____________
8. They endded the date with a kise! ____________ ____________

→ GK pages 28/29
→ EK pages 30/31

What do you remember?

Du musst aufpassen, wenn du sehr schnell Fahrrad fährst.	You must ______ when you're riding your bike very fast.	☐
In den USA sind alle staatlichen Schulen umsonst.	In the US all ______ are free.	☐
Glaubst du, dass du den Mathematiktest bestehen wirst?	Do you think you will ______ the Maths test?	☐
Die meisten Kinder kommen in die Grundschule, wenn sie sechs Jahre alt sind.	Most children start ______ when they are six years old.	☐
Die Spieler wagen es nicht, mit dem neuen Fußballkapitän an der Loyola High School zu streiten.	The players don't ______ to argue with the new ______ captain at Loyola High School.	☐ ☐
Kannst du mir bitte die weißen Tassen aus dem oberen Regal reichen?	Can you pass me the white cups from the ______ shelf, please?	☐
Ich möchte weniger Taschengeld für Zeitschriften ausgeben.	I want to spend ______ pocket money on magazines.	☐
Die erste Klasse in amerikanischen Mittelschulen ist oft die sechste Klasse.	The first grade in American ______ is often sixth grade.	☐

7 Phonetics

Read the words and then write them down correctly.

1. ['sɒkə] ______
2. [ˌpʌblɪk 'sku:l] ______
3. [deə] ______
4. [pɑ:s] ______
5. [teɪk 'keə] ______
6. ['mɪdl ˌsku:l] ______
7. ['ʌpə] ______
8. [elɪ'mentri ˌsku:l] ______

8 Rhyming words

Find a word (or two words) in the grid above that rhymes with a word below.

1. mess – ______
2. grass – ______
3. supper – ______
4. fair – ______, ______
5. rule – ______
6. lake – ______

→ GK pages 30/31
→ EK pages 32/33

What do you remember?	
Hast du schon den Apfelsaft bezahlt?	Have you already ________ the apple ________?
Unser Fußballteam und das Team der Paradise Valley High School sind Konkurrenten.	Our soccer team and the team of Paradise Valley High School are ________________.
Mein Traum ist es, Ballkönigin zu sein. Bitte stimmt für mich!	My dream is to be homecoming queen. Please ____________ for me!
Bist du wirklich ehrlich, wenn du mir sagst, dass ich diesen roten Anzug tragen kann?	Are you really being ____________ when you tell me that I can wear this red ____________?
Könnten Sie bitte mein Glas mit Wasser füllen?	Please could you ____________ my glass with water?
Eine Kneipe verkauft Getränke und manchmal sogar Essen.	A ____________ sells drinks and sometimes even food.
Die Ärmel an diesem Hemd sind viel zu lang. Ich sehe doof aus!	The ____________ on this shirt are much too long. I look silly!

9 Words and pictures

Look at these pictures and complete the sentences.

1. 

2. 

3. 

4. 

5. 

6. 

1. I met Kristy in the juice ____________ on Thursday.
2. I like this T-shirt but the ____________ are too short.
3. I love music shows on TV. I always ____________ my favourite singer.
4. Water is boring! But I really like orange ____________.
5. I had a hot date with Tom last night! And he even wore a ______!
6. Have you ____________ the bagels and cupcakes?

→ GK pages 30/31
→ EK page 33

What do you remember?

Wie peinlich, die einzige Person auf der Tanzfläche zu sein!	How embarrassing to be the only person on the ____________!
Mein Bruder hat ein Bild von einem Auto auf der Vorderseite seines T-Shirts.	My brother has a picture of a car on the ____________ of his T-shirt.
Meine Schwester sagt, sie wird lügen, wenn unsere Eltern versuchen, mehr über ihren Freund herauszufinden.	My sister says she will ____________ when our parents try to find out more about her boyfriend.
Jemand, der tollpatschig ist, lässt oft Sachen fallen.	Somebody who is ____________ often drops things.
David hat die Abstimmung fast zu leicht gewonnen. Glaubst du, er hat versucht sie zu manipulieren?	David won the ____________ almost too easily. Do you think he tried to ____________ it?
Im letzten Fußballspiel fiel der Kapitän hin und verletzte sich an der Schulter.	In the last soccer match the captain fell and hurt his ____________.
Deine E-Mail war wirklich gemein. Du hast meine Gefühle verletzt.	Your e-mail was really ____________. You've hurt my feelings.
„He, du Tollpatsch! Sei vorsichtig und zerbrich nichts!"	"____________! Be careful and don't break anything!"

10 Word search

Look for the nine words from the grid above. You will find them across → and down ↓.

C	R	I	N	Y	T	X	S	D	C	D	I
E	F	R	O	N	T	E	S	T	C	A	I
E	R	H	U	M	E	A	N	S	T	N	A
H	U	O	V	R	Y	I	O	R	D	C	H
E	Y	U	S	U	M	S	E	S	S	E	B
Y	W	C	L	U	M	S	Y	C	A	F	P
H	S	L	I	F	Y	A	A	K	R	L	I
J	S	D	E	L	I	D	E	D	S	O	X
A	V	R	N	V	O	T	Y	E	A	O	Q
C	O	S	H	O	F	I	X	A	T	R	S
Y	T	Z	Y	T	H	O	U	T	D	E	R
G	E	R	S	H	O	U	L	D	E	R	O

→ EK pages 28/32

What do you remember?

Gestern beim Cheerleading-Training war ich sehr verlegen, weil ich zweimal hingefallen bin!	Yesterday at ___________ practice I was very ___________ because I fell twice!
Hast du die Wolken gesehen? Heute wird es bestimmt regnen.	Have you seen the clouds? It will ___________ rain today.
Wenn ich den Schulabschluss gemacht habe, möchte ich meinen eigenen Laden eröffnen.	When I ___________, I want to ___________ my own shop.
Lasst uns versuchen, wieder guten Mutes zu sein, obwohl Matt einige verletzende Dinge zu uns gesagt hat.	Let's try to ___________, although Matt said some ___________ things to us.
Mein Bruder war direkt hinter mir in der Schlange und ich habe es nicht bemerkt!	My brother was ___________ behind me in the queue and I didn't notice!
Wenn du jemandem nicht glaubst, kannst du sagen: „Du machst Witze."	If you don't believe somebody, you can say, "___________."
„Jetzt haben wir stundenlang in dieser riesigen Einkaufspassage eingekauft! Wo kann ich einen Café latte bekommen?"	"Now we've been shopping for hours in this huge ___________! Where can I get a ___________?"
Es war nett von dir, mich zum Mittagessen einzuladen.	It was ___________ of you to invite me to lunch.
Wenn du dein Essen nicht magst, darfst du nicht laut „Igitt!" sagen.	If you don't like your food, you mustn't say "___________!" loudly.
Soll ich auf meinem Schulfoto wie ein Model posieren?	Should I ___________ like a model for my school photo?

11 Letter puzzle

Put the German words into English.

1. wieder guten Mutes sein
2. Igitt!
3. eröffnen
4. direkt
5. bestimmt
6. den Schulabschluss machen
7. Café latte
8. verletzend

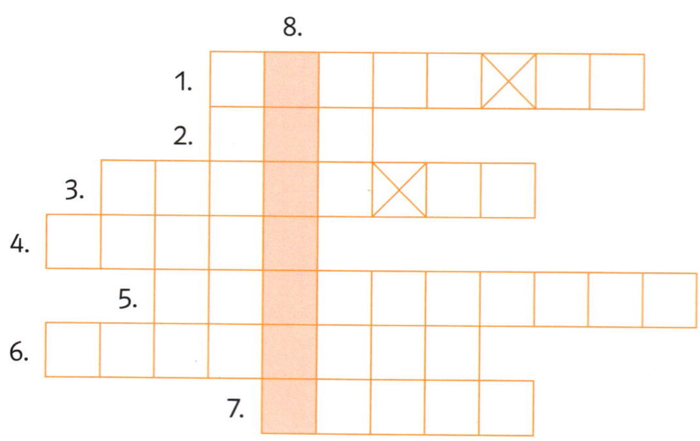

→ EK pages 32/33

What do you remember?

„Hast du den Tratsch über den Fußballkapitän gehört?“	“Have you heard the ______ about the soccer captain?”
„Dieser Typ mit den langen braunen Haaren, Adam?“	“That ______ with the long brown hair, Adam?”
„Ja! Ich habe einige interessante Geschichten über ihn gehört, als ich in der Turnhalle trainierte. Ich hing mit einigen seiner Freunde rum.“	“Yes! I heard some interesting stories about him while I was ______ in the gym. I was ______ with some of his friends.”
„Was hast du gehört? Ich weiß, dass er eine neue Band gegründet hat.“	“What did you hear? I know that he has started a new ______.”
„Ja, hat er! Seine Freunde sagten, dass die Musik schrecklich ist! Adam hat jetzt Fußball aufgegeben und verschwendet seine Zeit mit dieser Musik.“	“Yes, he has! His friends were saying that the music is ______! Adam has now given up soccer and is ______ his time on that music.”
„Wirklich? Das glaube ich überhaupt nicht. Diese Jungs möchten nur gern tratschen.“	“Really? I don't believe that ______. Those boys just like to ______.”
Es ist wichtig, sich vor dem Sport aufzuwärmen.	It is important to ______ before you do sports.
Als Helen mit Ben tanzte, ist er auf ihren Fuß getreten.	When Helen danced with Ben, he ______ on her foot.
Was für ein Schuss – leider verfehlte er das Tor!	What a shot – I'm afraid it ______ the goal!

12 Missing letters

Add the letters and complete the words from the grid.

1. _ _ _ t i _ g
2. _ w _ _ _
3. _ _ s _ _ p
4. _ a _ _ _ _
5. a _ _ _ l
6. m _ _ _ _ d
7. _ _ n _ _ n _ _ _ o _ _ d
8. _ _ a i _ _ _ _
9. _ _ y
10. _ _ n _
11. s _ _ _ p _ _

What do you remember?		
Ich habe gestern Abend auf der Party eine Zigarette probiert.	I tried a ______________ at the party last night.	☐
Mein Bruder machte letztes Jahr den Schulabschluss und ist jetzt an der Universität.	My brother ______________ from high school last year and now he is at ______________.	☐ ☐
Ich habe einen Fehler gemacht, als ich den ganzen Kuchen aß. Jetzt fühle ich mich schlecht.	I made a ______________ by eating all the cake. Now I feel ______________.	☐ ☐
Du kannst ab 19 h jederzeit zu meiner Party kommen.	You can come to my party ______________ after 7 p.m.	☐
Beim Umzug sah ich einen ziemlich bunten Drachen!	At the parade I saw a pretty ______________ dragon!	☐
Für einige wilde Tiere ist das Überleben schwierig.	______________ is difficult for some wild animals.	☐
Können wir uns nach der vierten Unterrichtsstunde im Schulhof treffen?	Can we meet in the playground after fourth ______________?	☐
Wir müssen die Bilder den richtigen Wörtern zuordnen.	We have to ______________ the pictures with the correct words.	☐
Sind Bleistifte echt voll Blei?	Are pencils really full of ______________?	☐
Du darfst nach dem Unterricht zur Toilette gehen.	You ______________ go to the toilet after class.	☐

13 Questions and answers

Match the questions with the correct answers.

1. Do these shoes match my suit?
2. Are you ill?
3. Has she graduated from high school already?
4. May I come to see you?
5. Do you want a cigarette?

a. Yes. I ate some bad fish. Big mistake!
b. Of course! You're welcome at any time.
c. Well, maybe they are a bit too colorful.
d. No, I don't smoke.
e. Yes, she's at university now.

14 Odd man out

Which word doesn't fit? Underline it.

1. alcohol – vegetables – tobacco – drugs
2. red – purple – colorful – blue
3. homecoming – yearbook – cheerleader – A-levels
4. cigarette – coke – water – juice

Revision

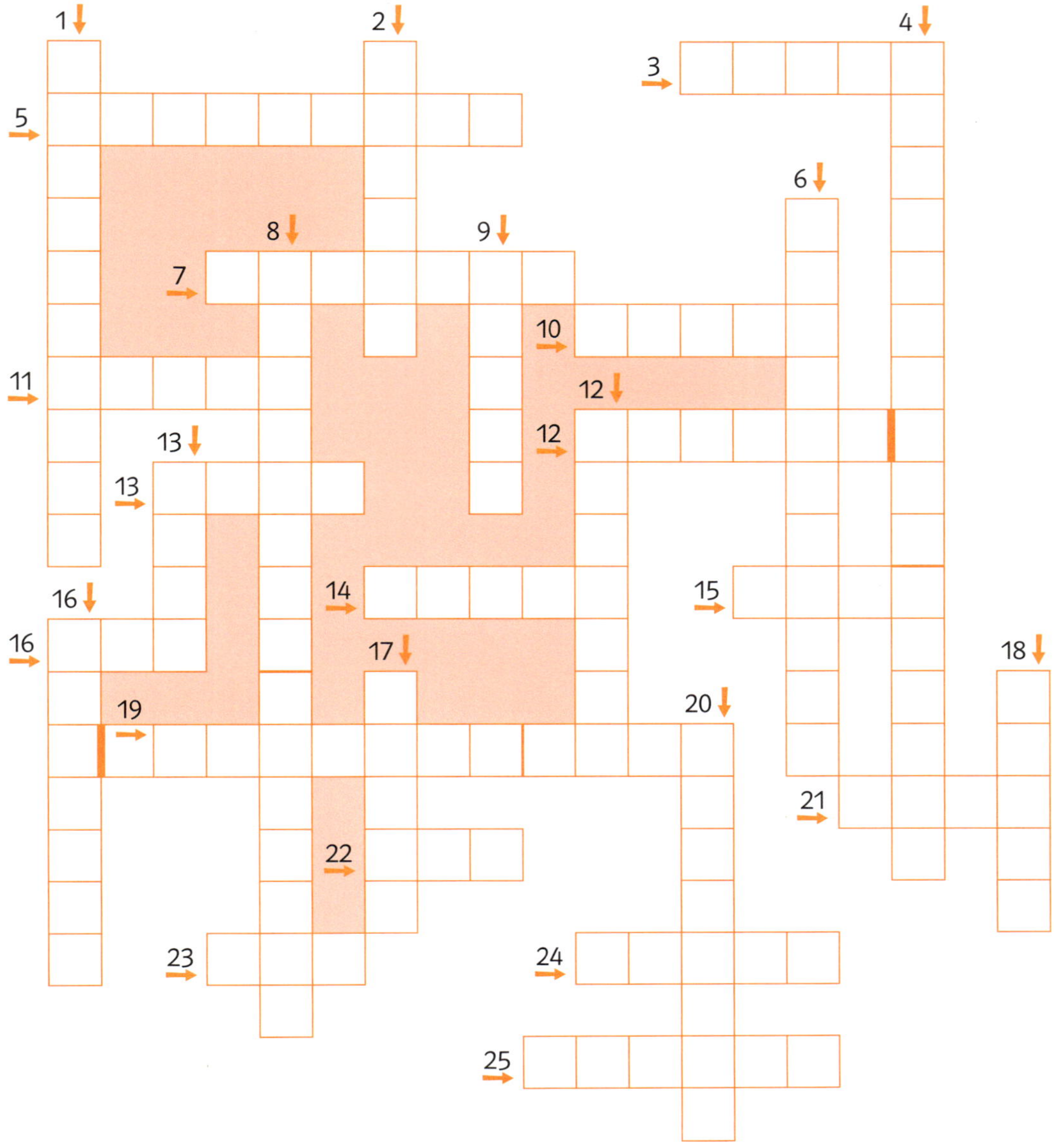

Across →

3. Klasse
5. jeder
7. Abwesenheit
10. Saft
11. dennoch
12. Anzeige
13. riskieren
14. Banden
15. bestehen
16. lügen
19. neueste Nachrichten
21. abstimmen
22. Ärmel
23. abschließen
24. Jugendtreffen
25. ehrlich

Down ↓

1. Erlaubnis
2. Fußball
4. Grundschule
6. Cheerleader
8. Gesellschaftstanz
9. singen
12. toll
13. Verabredung
16. glücklicherweise
17. Konkurrent/Konkurrentin
18. Kleidung
20. Schulter

→ GK pages 40/41
→ EK pages 42/43

What do you remember?	
Im Wissenschaftsmuseum können wir Erfindungen und Roboter sehen.	At the Science Museum we can see ______ and ______ .
Ich habe eine Sendung über eine Weltraumstation gesehen. Die Astronautin musste die Ausrüstung reparieren. Das war schwierig!	I saw a programme about a ______ . The ______ had to repair the ______ . That was hard!
Hast du genug Platz im Auto?	Have you got enough ______ in the car?
Die Erde sieht aus dem Weltall sehr klein aus.	______ looks very small from ______ .
Es ist klug, dein Gewicht genau zu überwachen, wenn du eine Diät machst.	It is ______ to ______ your weight exactly when you go on a diet.
Die Monster in diesem Computerspiel sehen echt aus, sind aber virtuell.	The monsters in this computer game look real but are ______ .
Mein Opa ist sehr krank. Nur ein neuer Herzschrittmacher kann ihm jetzt helfen.	My grandad is very sick. Only a new ______ can help him now.
Manchmal ist ein Traum besser als die Wirklichkeit.	Sometimes a dream is better than ______ .
Ein Bauer braucht seinen Traktor, um die Felder zu pflügen.	A farmer needs his ______ to ______ the fields.

1 Find the words

Find the words from above and write them in the correct places.

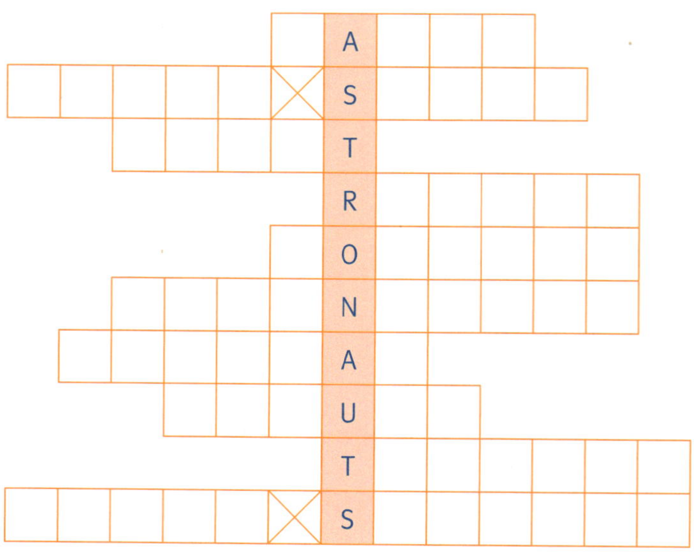

→ GK pages 40/41
→ EK pages 42/43

What do you remember?		
Kannst du das Wetter von morgen vorhersagen?	Can you ____________ tomorrow's weather?	☐
Hast du die Fernbedienung für den Fernseher gesehen?	Have you seen the TV ____________?	☐
Unsere neue Raumfähre erforscht gerade den Planeten Mars.	Our new ____________ is just ____________ the ____________ Mars.	☐☐ ☐
Die Kinder fanden eine Bombe aus dem letzten Krieg. Glücklicherweise versuchten sie nicht, sie zu entschärfen!	The children found a ____________ from the last war. Luckily they didn't try to ____________ it!	☐ ☐
Das ist ein sehr modernes Handy. Sogar meine kleine Schwester kann es bedienen.	This is a very ____________ mobile. Even my little sister can ____________ it.	☐ ☐
Die Menschen müssen sich gut um die Erde kümmern. Wir können ohne sie nicht existieren!	____________ must look well after the earth. We can't ____________ without it!	☐ ☐
Für ihr Forschungsprojekt muss Sarah viele Experimente machen.	For her ____________ project Sarah has to do a lot of experiments.	☐
Käse ist ein Nebenprodukt der Milch.	Cheese is a ____________ from milk.	☐
Kannst du deinen Hund hier im Park nicht unter Kontrolle halten?	Can't you keep ____________ of your dog here in the park?	☐
Ein Satellit bewegt sich um die Erde herum.	A ____________ moves around the earth.	☐

2 The correct word

Underline the correct word to complete the sentences.

1. Quick! It's an emergency! We must *(operate/defuse/forecast)* the bomb!
2. Where is the remote *(control/shuttle/satellite)* for the DVD player?
3. She's a scientist. She does *(control/equipment/research)* at the university.
4. I want to be an astronaut and *(exist/explore/expect)* other planets.
5. This invention is a *(fall off/hands off/spin-off)* of space technology.
6. The Americans sent a very *(modern/honest/attractive)* satellite into space.
7. Can you *(forecast/wish/pledge)* the weather? – That's easy. Rain, rain, rain!
8. Robots are very smart. But *(jerks/pacemakers/humans)* are smarter!

→ GK page 42
→ EK page 44

What do you remember?		
Ein Kühlschrank hält das Essen kühl.	A ____________ keeps food cool.	☐
An einem Tag wie heute trocknen nasse Kleider draußen schnell.	On a day like today wet clothes ____________ quickly outside.	☐
Mein Handy macht Musik, wenn ich es einschalte.	My ____________ plays music when I ____________ it ________.	☐ ☐
Ein Computer braucht Strom, deshalb kannst du ihn während eines Stromausfalls nicht benutzen.	A computer needs ____________ so you can't use it during a ____________.	☐ ☐
Lauras neuer Kühlschrank ist sehr high-tech.	Laura's new refrigerator is very ____________.	☐
Anna fand den Mathetest leicht. Sie ist echt klug!	Anna found the Maths test easy. She's really ____________!	☐

3 Blackout!

Put in the words from the grid.

It was terrible on Sunday morning. There was a ____________ and we had no ____________. I couldn't wash my hair because I need to ____________ it well in this really cold weather. So I went to the ____________ for a drink of milk, but the milk was warm and quite yukky. Then I tried to ____________ my ____________, but it was broken! In the end, I read a book. At least that was an ____________ idea. But I guess we need electricity for almost everything in our ____________ world!

4 Definition

Tick the right definition for each word.

1. intelligent
   - ☐ a. interesting
   - ☐ b. rich
   - ☐ c. smart
2. cell phone
   - ☐ a. mobile
   - ☐ b. remote control
   - ☐ c. robot
3. blackout
   - ☐ a. There is suddenly no water.
   - ☐ b. There is suddenly no electricity.
   - ☐ c. There is suddenly no food.
4. refrigerator
   - ☐ a. Food stays warm inside it.
   - ☐ b. Food stays cool inside it.
   - ☐ c. It burns food.
5. electricity
   - ☐ a. a kind of alcohol
   - ☐ b. a kind of jewellery
   - ☐ c. a kind of power
6. high-tech home
   - ☐ a. a house with a lot of technology
   - ☐ b. a house with an old kitchen
   - ☐ c. a house with a big garden

→ EK page 44

What do you remember?

Unsere Waschmaschine hat angefangen zu lecken.	Our ________ has started to ________ .
Entferne bitte deine Haare aus dem Waschbecken!	________ your hair from the ________ , please!
Benutze keinen Stöpsel, wenn du eine Dusche nimmst, oder du wirst das Bad überschwemmen!	Don't use a ________ when you take a shower, or you will ________ the bathroom!
Dieser elektrische Roller wird von einer deutschen Firma gemacht.	This ________ kickboard is made ________ a German company.
Ich benutze den Wäschetrockner nur im Winter.	I only use the ________ in winter.
Bevor du Bohnen kochst, musst du sie waschen.	Before you ________ beans, you must wash them.
Wenn es regnet, sollte das Wasser schnell ablaufen.	When it rains, the water should ________ quickly.
Ich hätte diese E-Mail nicht öffnen sollen – jetzt ist mein PC vom Internet abgeschnitten!	I shouldn't have opened this e-mail – now my PC is ________ from the Internet!
Warum wurde der Wasserhahn im Bad nicht von einem Handwerker repariert?	Why wasn't the ________ in the bathroom repaired by a workman?

5 What can you say?

Match the two parts of the sentences.

1. You'll find the plug
2. Turn off the faucet
3. My father cut off the electricity
4. The washing machine
5. When mum cooks vegetable soup,

a. because it's flooding the bathroom!
b. in the sink.
c. is leaking.
d. I always remove the peas.
e. so I couldn't use the tumble drier.

6 Phonetics

Read the words. Then write them down correctly.

1. [ˌrʌn‿əˈweɪ] ________
2. [kʊk] ________
3. [kʌt‿ˈɒf] ________
4. [ɪˈlektrɪkl] ________
5. [ˈwɒʃɪŋ məˌʃiːn] ________
6. [sɪŋk] ________
7. [liːk] ________
8. [ˈtʌmbl ˌdraɪə] ________
9. [flʌd] ________

→ GK pages 44/45
→ EK pages 46/47

What do you remember?

Wir bewahren den Fön im Badezimmer auf.	We ______ the ______ in the bathroom.
Bitte pass auf, wenn du die Steckdose im Bad benutzt.	Please take care when you use the ______ in the bathroom.
Wenn du in ein anderes Land reist, kann ein Adapter sehr nützlich sein.	When you travel to another country, an ______ can be very ______.
Die Lampe im Flur braucht eine neue Glühbirne.	The ______ in the corridor needs a new ______.
Mein Essen ist kalt geworden. Kannst du es bitte für mich in die Mikrowelle stellen?	My food has become cold. Can you put it in the ______ for me, please?
Wenn ich mein Handy einschalte, passiert nichts. Es ist leer!	When I ______ my cell phone ______, nothing happens. It's ______!
Der Schalter für das Badezimmerlicht ist hinter dem Vorhang.	The ______ for the bathroom light is behind the ______.

7 Which word is it?

Choose the right word and complete the sentences.

1. Percy Spencer invented the ______.
2. The ______  in my bedroom are brand new!
3. In Britain, there are no ______  in the bathroom because people think it is dangerous.
4. – Have you got two dollars for a new ______  ?
5. – Yes, of course. Is it for the ______  on the table in the kitchen?
6. Oh no, the battery for my cell phone is ______! 

→ GK page 46
→ EK page 48

What do you remember?

Ohne den richtigen Code kannst du mein Schließfach nicht öffnen.	Without the correct ______ you can't open my locker.	☐
Bringt diese Dinge in die richtige Reihenfolge, vom Größten zum Kleinsten.	Put these things in the right ______, from biggest to smallest.	☐
Wenn du nicht genügend Schlaf bekommst, fühlst du dich schrecklich.	If you don't get enough ______, you will feel terrible.	☐
Ich muss einen frühen Zug nehmen, um pünktlich zur Arbeit zu kommen.	I need to take an early train to get to work ______.	☐
Ein belegtes Brot plus einem Getränk kostet fünf Euro.	A sandwich ______ a drink is five euros.	☐
Hast du das Warnschild an der Straße gesehen?	Have you seen the ______ sign on the road?	☐
Kann ich eine Aufnahme deines Konzerts von gestern Abend kaufen?	Can I buy a ______ of your concert last night?	☐
Hast du dir die Zähne geputzt?	Have you ______ your teeth?	☐
Vor Prüfungen gibt es immer viel Stress.	Before exams there is always a lot of ______.	☐

8 Jumbled crossword

Find the words and put them into the grid.

Across →
3. estsrs
6. no miet
8. eodc
9. granwin

Down ↓
1. dresbhu
2. slup
4. cregornid
5. peesl
7. drreo

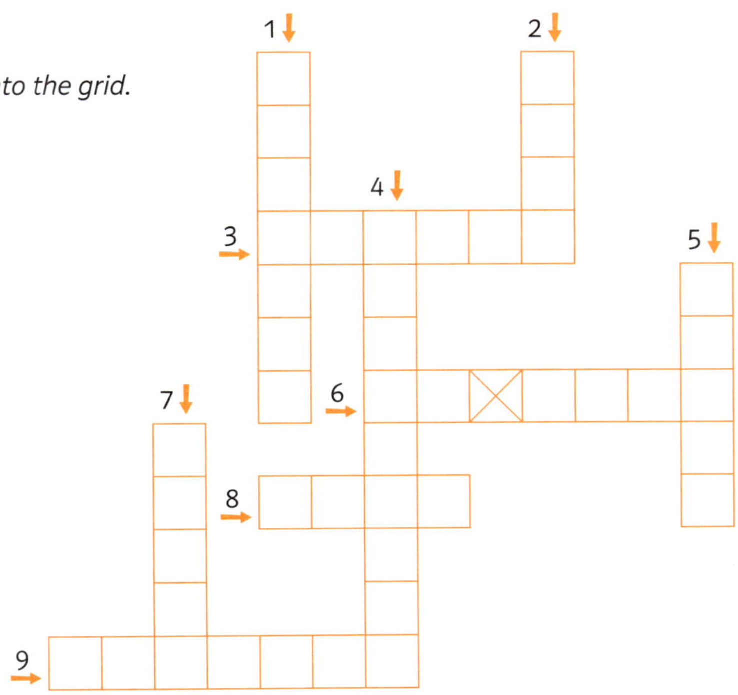

→ GK pages 48/49
→ EK pages 50/51

What do you remember?		
Die Berge in Kanada sind wunderschön.	The ______ in Canada are beautiful.	☐
Diese Fabrik hat mehr als 200 Angestellte.	This ______ has more than 200 ______.	☐ ☐
Wenn etwas rechtswidrig ist, tu es nicht!	If something is ______, don't do it!	☐
Ist das deine neue Brille? Sie sieht schön aus.	Are those your new ______? They look nice.	☐
Es gab eine Menge Spannung in dem Film gestern Abend, weil jeder geheime Pläne hatte!	There was a lot of ______ in the film last night because everybody had ______ plans!	☐ ☐
Als Hausaufgabe bitte bis zum Ende der Geschichte weiterlesen.	For homework, please read ______ to the end of the story.	☐
Ein Schauspieler braucht eine Agentin, die für ihn Arbeit findet.	An actor needs an ______ who finds him work.	☐
Als ich in Indien war, fühlte ich mich zunächst sehr fremd.	When I was in India, I felt very ______ at first.	☐

9 More letters than you need

You only need every third letter. The words are from the grid above.

1. poarhgbvekjnuyt ______
2. wlwzeoqnrcckalebhrzcs ______
3. loacblouimbembn ______
4. crsmguzasgrpoaeuhndesdfe ______
5. vgfeeacgckttuiogfriey ______
6. brmjjoscugbnsrtdsalkigbnlis ______

10 Find the mistakes

Find two mistakes in each sentence and correct the words.

1. His wife thinks he's a kop, but he is a seecret agent. ______ ______
2. I told him too go on. "No," he said. "It's illigul." ______ ______
3. "Do you where glases?" asked Mandy. ______ ______
4. "Have you seen the new movey about alean monsters?" ______ ______
5. "Yes, theirs lots of suspence in it!" ______ ______
6. He works at a factry in the mountans. ______ ______

→ GK pages 48/49
→ EK pages 50/51

What do you remember?		
Der See in der Nähe unseres Hauses ist 20 Meter breit.	The lake near our house is 20 metres ____________.	☐
Mein Bruder redet mit seinen Freunden gerne über politische Ideen.	My brother likes to talk about ____________ ideas with his friends.	☐
Ich habe keine Ahnung von Rechtsfragen!	I have no idea about ____________ questions!	☐
Wenn du Zahnschmerzen hast, geh zum Zahnarzt.	If you have a ____________, go to the ____________.	☐ ☐
Ein Leuchtfeuer kann man von Weitem sehen.	You can see a ____________ from far away.	☐
Hast du irgendeinen Schmerz gespürt, als du vom Fahrrad gefallen bist?	Did you feel any ____________ when you fell off your bike?	☐
Hast du gehört? Emma und Tom sind jetzt ein Paar.	Have you heard? Emma and Tom are now a ____________.	☐
Gestern stahl eine Bande von Räubern viel Schmuck im reichsten Viertel unserer Stadt.	Yesterday a ____________ of ____________ stole a lot of jewellery in our city's richest neighborhood.	☐ ☐

11 Word search

Look for all ten words from the grid.
You can find them across → and down ↓.

Q	U	L	D	C	V	J	S	C	A	A	T	R	S
T	F	E	F	T	E	T	H	H	E	R	A	V	E
O	V	G	L	F	L	A	R	E	K	T	T	E	A
O	B	A	A	R	E	P	T	B	O	A	T	A	B
T	I	L	T	O	I	F	Y	U	R	C	S	E	A
H	N	C	H	B	W	A	E	H	H	R	I	P	N
A	I	A	E	B	L	E	A	F	W	O	S	O	D
C	N	W	W	R	O	B	B	E	R	S	I	L	P
H	S	F	Q	L	I	N	T	E	O	S	I	I	S
E	P	A	A	I	N	K	I	E	U	L	L	T	S
P	A	I	N	E	R	E	R	T	L	O	S	I	Y
C	D	E	N	T	I	S	T	X	Q	U	I	C	I
U	I	B	A	N	R	R	E	E	C	O	O	A	U
P	L	E	G	A	E	E	C	C	O	U	P	L	E
L	A	C	V	R	R	I	S	Y	T	I	U	C	A

→ GK pages 48/49

What do you remember?

Meine Chefin hat einen Witz gemacht, aber ich habe ihn nicht verstanden.	My ________ made a joke but I didn't ____________ .
Die Sonne ist im Zentrum unseres Sonnensystems.	The sun is in the centre of our ____________________ .
Lea ist mit ihrer Note nicht zufrieden. Tim ist mit seiner Note auch nicht zufrieden.	Lea isn't pleased with her grade. Tim ________ pleased with his grade ____________ .
Du bekommst ein Stück Pizza für ungefähr vier Dollar.	You get a ________ of pizza for ________ four dollars.
Kennst du eine gute Agentur für Schauspieler?	Do you know a good ______________ for actors?
Man kann ein echtes Raumschiff im Museum sehen.	You can see a real ________________ in the museum.
Die neue Solarlampe im Garten sieht toll aus!	The new ________ lamp in the garden looks great!
Die vier Hunde nebenan machen mir wirklich Angst.	The four dogs next door really ______________ me.
Ich gehe jeden Tag am Bahnhof vorbei.	I ________ the train station everyday.
Vor drei Jahren konnte ich erst wenig Englisch sprechen.	Three years ago I could only speak a ____________ English.

12 What kind of word?

Put the words from the grid into the correct column. Find at least two words for each column.

Verb	Noun
Adjective	**Other**

→ EK page 50

What do you remember?

In den USA darf man ohne Sozialversicherungsnummer nicht arbeiten.	You can't work in the US without a ____________.
In einem Flugzeug ist die Sicherheit aller Passagiere sehr wichtig.	In a plane the ____________ of all passengers is very important.
Ich würde gerne die Party von gestern Abend aus meinem Gedächtnis löschen!	I would like to ____________ last night's party from my ____________!
Am Flughafen wurde mein Visum zweimal kontrolliert.	At the airport my ____________ was checked twice.
Bist du eigentlich schon in New York gewesen?	Have you ____________ been to New York already?
Jedes Mal wenn ich verdeckt arbeite, muss ich meine Haare und meine Kleidung verändern.	Every time I work ____________, I have to change my hair and my clothes.
In Australien haben Wissenschaftler einen riesigen Käfer entdeckt.	In Australia scientists have ____________ a huge ____________.
Im Supermarkt gab es eine zehn Meter lange Schlange. Das war die Hölle!	There was a ten metre queue at the supermarket. That was ____________!
Kinderarmut ist ein großes soziales Thema.	Child poverty is a big ____________ topic.
Die Polizei erwischte meinen Bruder nicht, als er illegal ein Auto fuhr. Das war ein sehr großes Risiko!	The police didn't catch my brother when he drove a car illegally. That was a very big ____________!

13 Questions and answers

Match the questions with the correct answers.

1. What is your social security number?
2. Is he actually a robber?
3. Should I worry about our security?
4. Do you have a good memory in new social groups?
5. Is that animal a risk?
6. What did you discover?
7. Do I need a visa for Australia?

a. Yes, you do!
b. Nothing. Somebody has erased all the information.
c. No, it's only a little bug.
d. No, he's an undercover agent.
e. Yes, I can remember faces very well!
f. It's 987-65-4321.
g. Yes. There's a lot of crime. It's hell for normal people.

→ EK pages 50/51

What do you remember?

Als ich in die USA flog, dauerte die ganze Reise zehn Stunden.	When I flew to the US, the ______ journey took ten hours.
Während ich an Bord des Flugzeugs war, hat sich die Besatzung prima um mich gekümmert.	While I was ______ the plane, the ______ were looking after me brilliantly.
Kannst du beschreiben, was du in der Entfernung siehst?	Can you ______ what you can see in the ______?
Gesten Abend habe ich einen seltsamen Gegenstand am Himmel gesehen. Er war V-förmig und sehr schnell.	Last night I saw a strange ______ in the sky. It was ______ and very fast.
Ein Fluglotse muss berichten, was er am Himmel sieht.	An ______ must ______ what he sees in the sky.
Als ich den Unfall sah, war mein erster Gedanke, sofort die Polizei anzurufen.	When I saw the accident, my first ______ was to call the police at once.
Dieses Problem ist nicht einfach, deshalb brauchen wir unseren besten Ermittler, um es zu klären.	This problem isn't ______, so we need our best ______ to sort it out.

14 Which word is it?

Complete the sentences.

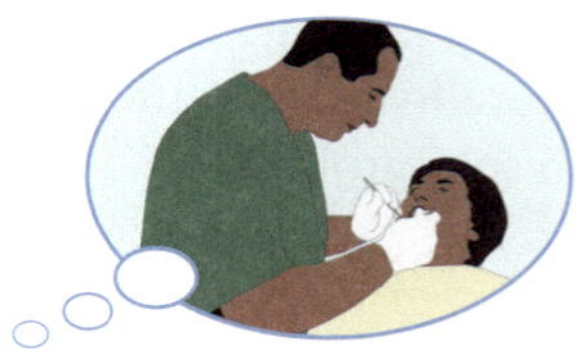

1. I'm so hungry! Don't give me just a piece of this pizza – I want the ______ thing!
2. Even the ______ of the ______ scares me!
3. Each physical thing can be described as an ______.

4. In the documentary they described the work of an ______.
5. Another word for 'easy' is ______.
6. For a detective story you need at least one bad guy and one ______, like Sherlock Holmes.

7. On a plane the pilots are also a part of the ______.
8. I can't believe that about 350,000 different ______ exist on our planet!

What do you remember?

Meine neuen Schuhe kosteten 50 Euro.	My new shoes ______ 50 euros.	☐
Plattenläden sind oft schwierig zu finden.	______ shops are often difficult to find.	☐
Wenn du einen hohen IQ hast, denken die Leute, dass du sehr intelligent bist.	If you have a high ______, people think that you are very intelligent.	☐
Ich schreibe gerade einen Bericht über Roboter für unsere Schülerzeitung.	I'm just writing a ______ about robots for our school paper.	☐
Ich habe mein Handy fallen gelassen und nun versuche ich, es zu reparieren.	I've dropped my cell phone and now I'm trying to ______ it.	☐
Meine neue Wohnung hat drei Schlafzimmer.	My new ______ has three bedrooms.	☐
Hey, dein nasser Regenschirm tropft auf den Boden!	Hey, your wet umbrella is ______ on the floor!	☐
Glücklicherweise konnte Jane ihr Auto auf der verschneiten Straße beherrschen.	Luckily Jane could ______ her car on the snowy road.	☐
Ich hätte gerne eine Badewanne, aber wir haben nur eine Dusche.	I would like to have a ______ but we only have a shower.	☐

15 Questions and answers

Match the questions with the correct answers.

1. Do you like this apartment?
2. Can you fix my refrigerator, please?
3. How much did this cool record cost?
4. Did you read this report about elephants?
5. Can you control the temperature?
6. Is the faucet in the bathtub still dripping?

a. Yes. Is it too hot?
b. Maybe. What's wrong with it?
c. No, because the bathroom doesn't have a bathtub.
d. No, a workman has repaired it.
e. Yes. It says they have a very high IQ.
f. Nothing. It was free with a magazine.

What do you remember?	
Bevor du Bohnen kochst, musst du sie waschen.	Before you ______ beans, you must wash them.
Versuch die Titel zu lesen, während du an den Bücherregalen vorbeigehst.	Try to read the titles ______ you pass the book shelves.
Ein Motel ist oft billiger als ein Hotel.	A ______ is often cheaper than a hotel.
Der Stöpsel hält das Wasser im Waschbecken.	The ______ keeps the water in the ______.
Der Wasserhahn in der Küche tropfte die ganze Nacht.	The ______ in the kitchen dripped all night.
Was war die genaue Zeit des Unfalls?	What was the ______ time of the accident?
Magst du einen Kirsch- oder einen Erdbeer-Milchshake? Du hast die Wahl.	Would you like a cherry or a strawberry milkshake? It's your ______.
Heute Abend muss ich auf meine zwei kleinen Brüder aufpassen – das ist keine leichte Aufgabe!	Tonight I have to look after my two little brothers – that's not an easy ______!

16 Odd man out

Which word doesn't fit? Underline it.

1. faucet – bathtub – bed – shower
2. work – task – homework – fun
3. apartment – refrigerator – home – motel
4. exact – about – around – nearly
5. love – stress – pacemaker – pain
6. to clean – to cook – to wash – to explore

17 Missing letters

Add the missing letters and complete the words from the grid.

1. _ s
2. _ x _ _ _
3. c _ _ _ _ _
4. _ _ _ _ l
5. _ o _ _
6. _ _ s _
7. _ a _ _ _ _
8. s _ _ _
9. _ _ u _

What do you remember?

Regen tropft vom Dach auf meinen Kopf.	Rain is ____________ from the roof onto my head.	☐
Morgen um 8 Uhr wird die NASA ihr neues Raumschiff starten.	Tomorrow at 8 a.m. NASA will ____________ their new ____________.	☐ ☐
Oh nein, ich habe mein neues Schulbuch verloren!	Oh no, I've lost my new ____________!	☐
Die Länge des Amazonas ist etwa 6500 km.	The ____________ of the Amazon is about 6,500 km.	☐
Pass auf, da liegt ein Telefonkabel auf dem Boden.	Take care, there is a phone ____________ lying on the floor.	☐
In den Ferien sind alle Schulen geschlossen.	All schools are ____________ during the holidays.	☐
Die meisten Leute stellen ihren Kühlschrank in die Küche.	Most people put their ____________ in the kitchen.	☐
Hast du jemals einen wissenschaftlichen Bericht gelesen?	Have you ever read a ____________ report?	☐
Mia kann dein Auto reparieren; sie ist eine tolle Mechanikerin.	Mia can fix your car; she's a great ____________.	☐
Ich konnte mein Pferd erst nach vielen Reitstunden richtig führen.	I could only ____________ my horse correctly after many riding lessons.	☐
Welche Behörde hilft Leuten, die einen neuen Job suchen?	Which ____________ helps people who are looking for a new job?	☐

18 Word search

Look for the 12 words from the grid. You can find them across → and down ↓.

E	P	E	D	R	A	I	M	V	L	E	C	W	O
P	L	P	R	W	T	E	X	T	B	O	O	K	H
S	A	K	Z	L	Y	R	S	T	I	L	N	D	T
C	L	O	S	E	D	H	I	P	E	L	T	B	Y
I	A	B	O	N	Z	O	D	R	G	O	R	P	N
E	U	V	A	G	E	N	C	Y	A	E	O	K	T
N	N	S	R	T	N	S	S	R	P	Y	L	N	O
T	C	A	L	H	E	D	R	I	P	P	I	N	G
I	H	P	U	S	M	R	R	G	L	I	T	C	A
F	R	I	D	G	E	C	G	U	A	V	O	T	M
I	G	F	Y	B	N	M	E	C	H	A	N	I	C
C	O	R	D	R	S	P	A	C	E	S	H	I	P

Revision

Across →

1. Paar
3. Weltraum
5. bedienen
9. Raumfähre
10. Ausstattung
13. Warnung
15. Strom
16. trocknen
17. Zahnschmerzen
19. Räuber/Räuberin
22. fremd
23. Roboter

Down ↓

1. Handy
2. Fön
4. Verschlüsselung
6. Vorhang
7. unrechtmäßig
8. Spannung
9. Stress
11. Traktor
12. rechtlich
14. Glühbirne
16. entschärfen
17. einschalten
18. nützlich
20. Bombe
21. Vertreter/Vertreterin

→ GK pages 56/57
→ EK pages 60/61

What do you remember?

Letzten Sommer habe ich einen Nationalpark in den USA besucht.	Last summer I visited a ______________ in the US.
Auf dem Land ist die Landschaft wunderschön.	In the country the ______________ is beautiful.
Einige Volksstämme in den USA leben in Reservaten.	Some __________ in the US live on ______________.
Man kann ein Schiff nehmen und durch die Schlucht fahren.	You can take a boat through the ______________.
Wenn du etwas über Rinderhirten erfahren möchtest, kannst du auf einer Ranch wohnen.	If you want to learn about ______________, you can stay on a ______________.
Meine Fahrt dauerte fünf Stunden, weil es so viele Lastwagen auf der Bundesstraße gab.	My journey took five hours because there were so many ______________ on the ______________.
Ein heiliger Ort ist für manche Leute etwas sehr Besonderes.	A __________ place is something very special for some people.

1 My day in my dad's truck

Choose the right word and complete the sentences.

1. My dad drives a large ______________ to take T-shirts, jeans and other clothes to the stores.

2. I went with him last week. First we drove past a huge ______________.
3. My dad told me that it is a reservation and that a ______________ lives there.

4. Then we drove past a big ranch. "Do you know how many ______________ work there?" I asked my dad.
5. An hour later we were on the ______________ on our way back home.

6. What a brilliant day! I really want to do this again and see some more great ______________!

→ GK pages 56/57
→ EK pages 60/61

What do you remember?

Dieser Kuchen hat fabelhaft geschmeckt, oder? 	This cake tasted ______, didn't it?
Würdest du gerne eines Tages Geld in einem Casino gewinnen?	Would you like to win some money at a ______ one day?
Manchmal muss ein Lastwagenfahrer die ganze Nacht durch fahren.	Sometimes a ______ has to drive all night long.
Nur die besten Cowboys können ein Rodeo gewinnen.	Only the best cowboys can win a ______.
Die Autobahn 90 in den USA ist fast 5000 km lang.	______ 90 in the US is nearly 5,000 km long.
Das *Empire State Building* ist eine berühmte Sehenswürdigkeit. 	The Empire State Building is a famous ______.
Ich wusste nicht, dass deine Mama Motorrad fahren kann.	I didn't know that your mum can ride a ______.
Ich brauche echt eine Pause – lass uns an der nächsten Imbissstube anhalten!	I really need a break – let's stop at the next ______!
Schiffe transportieren Waren aus den USA nach Europa.	Ships ______ ______ from the US to Europe.

2 The correct word

Underline the correct word to complete the sentences.

1. I don't want to cook tonight. What about going to the new *(diner/trucker/dime)* on West Street?
2. On *(International/Internet/Interstate)* 75 you can travel from Florida to Michigan.
3. Las Vegas is famous for its *(casinos/cinemas/castles)*.
4. A trucker's job is to *(travel/transport/try)* goods.
5. I visited the sacred reservation yesterday. It was *(formal/fabulous/dizzy)*!
6. Have you visited the Grand Canyon? You must! It's a fantastic *(smell/sound/sight)*.
7. "Does the man ride a *(motorbike/ship/refrigerator)*?" little Sophie asked her mother.
8. "No," her mother answered. "He rides a horse at the *(homecoming/rodeo/movies)*."

→ GK page 58

What do you remember?		
Der Bauernhof unserer Freunde ist fünf Morgen groß.	Our friends' farm is five ______ big.	☐
Pferde machen meinem Freund Angst, deshalb holt er mich nicht von der Reitschule ab!	Horses scare my boyfriend, so he doesn't pick me up from ______ school!	☐
Gestern Abend schaute ich mir einen coolen Western im Fernsehen an.	Last night I watched a cool ______ on TV.	☐
Junge und alte Leute genießen Square Dance.	Young and old people enjoy a ______.	☐
Im Sommer frisst das Vieh viel Gras.	In the summer the ______ eat a lot of grass.	☐
Von der Spitze dieses Hügels kannst du sehr weit sehen.	You can see very far from the top of this ______.	☐
Ich möchte gerne ein Pferd besitzen, weil Reiten mein Lieblingshobby ist.	I'd like to ______ a horse because ______ ______ is my favourite hobby.	☐☐
Nach unserem Spaziergang waren meine Schuhe staubig.	After our walk my shoes were ______.	☐

3 Definition

Tick the right definition for each word.

1. cattle
   - ☐ a. trucks
   - ☐ b. dogs
   - ☐ c. cows
2. square dance
   - ☐ a. western dance
   - ☐ b. dance from New York
   - ☐ c. modern dance
3. hill
   - ☐ a. small mountain
   - ☐ b. kind of truck
   - ☐ c. kind of tribe
4. to own
   - ☐ a. to be
   - ☐ b. to buy
   - ☐ c. to have
5. 150,000 acres
   - ☐ a. a lot of money
   - ☐ b. a lot of land
   - ☐ c. a long distance
6. riding
   - ☐ a. travelling by horse
   - ☐ b. travelling by plane
   - ☐ c. travelling on foot

4 The cowboy

What is the cowboy saying? Write it down.

____

____

____

[wiː lʌv ˈaʊə ræntʃ! wiːv ˈgɒt sɪks ˈθaʊznd ˈeɪkəz. ɪts fænˈtæstɪk fɔː ˈhɔːsbæk ˌraɪdɪŋ.]

→ GK page 58

What do you remember?		
Warum trittst du nicht auch dem neuen Schwimmklub bei? Ich werde das sicher tun, egal was passiert.	Why don't you also ______________ the new swimming club? I certainly will, ______________ happens.	☐ ☐
Man braucht viel Geschick, wenn man an einem Viehtrieb teilnehmen will.	You need a lot of ______________ if you want to take part in a ______________.	☐ ☐
Hast du das Einfangen der Rinder mit dem Lasso auf einer Ranch gelernt?	Did you learn ______________ on a ranch?	☐
Ein Parkaufseher weiß viel über Tiere.	A ______________ knows a lot about animals.	☐
Es gibt einen tiefen See etwa 20 Minuten von hier.	There is a ______________ lake about 20 minutes away.	☐
Möchten Sie eine Busfahrt machen? Sie kostet nur zehn Dollar!	Would you like to ______________? It's only ten dollars!	☐
Es macht Spaß, Lieder um ein Lagerfeuer herum zu singen.	It's fun to sing songs around a ______________.	☐
Ein Maultier ist ein sehr starkes Tier.	A ______________ is a very strong animal.	☐

5 More letters than you need

You only need every third letter. The words are from the grid above.

1. porlkodjpnaigmnlkg ______________
2. klcmeanmmlepdgfouietrase ______________
3. fndouejhenmp ______________
4. jkmhiujklsbe ______________
5. zcsackeeipklvbl ______________
6. bnwanhmaabgtwdeffvpeedfr ______________

6 Our visit to the ranch

Put in the correct words.

cowboys • skill • roping • campfire • cattle drive • bus tour • join • acres • whatever

On Friday we are taking a ______________ to a ranch which is 10,000 ______________ big. At the ranch there will be a lot to learn, for example ______________ at the ______________. I hope we can do it – ______________ we learn, we will certainly need a lot of ______________! In the evening we'll ______________ the ______________ and sing western songs together around the ______________. That sounds like a cool day, doesn't it?

→ EK pages 62/63

What do you remember?

Macht das Lagerfeuer nicht zu nahe am Wald!	Don't make the ____________ too close to the ____________ !
Während unseres Urlaubs in den Bergen vermisste ich das Surfen!	During our holidays in the mountains I ____________ surfing!
Bei unserer Reise war alles inklusive, also ohne zusätzliche Kosten.	Our trip was ____________ , so without any extra ____________ .
Die Temperatur erreichte ein Minimum von 2°C.	The temperature reached a ____________ of 2°C.
Kennst du die kleine Hütte im Wald?	Do you know the little ____________ in the ____________ ?
Du musst im nächsten Spiel vier Tore schießen! – Auf keinen Fall!	You have to score four goals in the next match! – ____________ !
Mit meinem neuen Hut sehe ich aus wie ein echter Camper.	With my new hat I look like a real ____________ .
Die Unterwasserwelt in Australien ist spannend.	The ____________ world in Australia is exciting.
Ich würde gern mehr über Fotografie erfahren. Gibt es bald einen neuen Kurs?	I'd like to learn more about ____________ . Will there be a new ____________ soon?

7 Jumbled crossword

Find the words and put them into the grid.

Across →

1. preamc
3. isms tou
5. tresof
7. treadwernu

Down ↓

1. stoc
2. pragtoyhoph
3. ummmnii
4. dwoo
6. banci

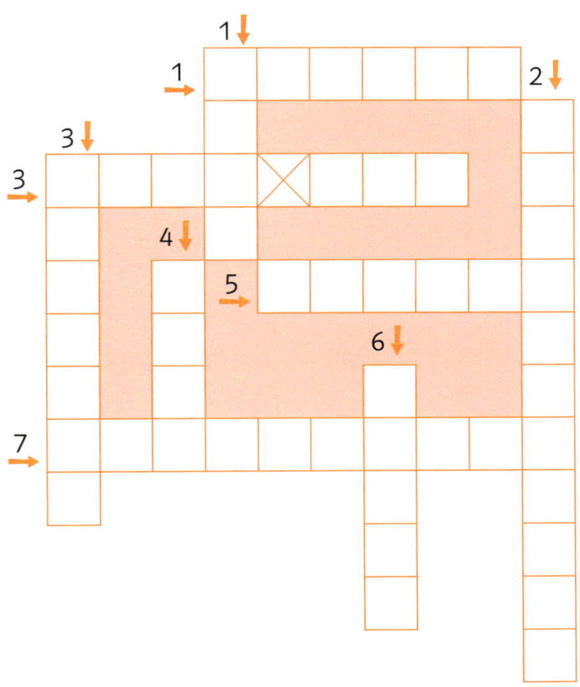

→ EK pages 62/63

What do you remember?		
Es ist gut, mit einer Beraterin über Probleme zu reden.	It is good to speak to a ______________ about problems.	☐
Wir werden Ihnen Fotos unseres Hotels per E-Mail schicken. Im März können wir Ihnen einen speziellen Preis anbieten.	We will ______________ you photos of our hotel. In March we can ______________ you a special price.	☐ ☐
Sind Sie mutig genug, um Rafting auszuprobieren? Das Wildwasser kann gefährlich sein!	Are you brave enough to try ______________? The ______________ can be dangerous!	☐ ☐
Wir sahen auf unserem Spaziergang Tierspuren, konnten sie aber nicht identifizieren.	We saw animal ______________ on our walk, but couldn't ______________ them.	☐ ☐
Oh nein, ich habe meinen neuen Bogen mitgenommen, aber meine Pfeile vergessen!	Oh no, I've brought my new ______________, but forgotten my ______________!	☐ ☐
Diese Fabrik stellt Papier her.	This factory ______________ paper.	☐
Vermisst du die Natur, wenn du in der Stadt lebst?	Do you miss ______________ when you live in the city?	☐
Was sind die Vor- und Nachteile eines Campingurlaubs?	What are the ______________ of a camping holiday?	☐

8 What's the word?

Read the definition and then write down the correct word from the grid above.

1. To send a message on your computer: ______________
2. A sign that an animal has left behind on the ground: ______________
3. Robin Hood could use these very well: ______________
4. Wild plants and animals: ______________
5. To ask somebody if they would like something: ______________
6. The good sides and the bad sides of something: ______________
7. It's the job of this person to advise and help other people: ______________
8. To make goods: ______________

→ GK pages 60/61
→ EK pages 64/65

What do you remember?		
Der 3. Oktober ist in Deutschland ein Feiertag.	October 3rd is a ____________ in Germany.	☐
Es ist nicht immer kostenlos, eine Hotline anzurufen.	It isn't always free to call a ____________.	☐
Ich brauche jetzt wirklich mein Abendessen. Können wir am nächsten Rastplatz bitte anhalten?	I really need my ____________ now. Can we please stop at the next ____________?	☐ ☐
Was hast du gemacht, als du ohne Telefon gestrandet warst?	What did you do when you were ____________ without a phone?	☐
Letzten Sommer war unser Flugzeug um zwei Stunden verspätet und es gab ein großes Durcheinander am Flughafen.	Last summer our plane was ____________ for two hours and there was a big ____________ at the airport.	☐ ☐
Fahr langsamer, da ist schon die Ausfahrt!	Drive more slowly, there's the ____________ already!	☐
An heißen Tagen gibt es auf den Highways viele Autopannen.	On hot days there are many ____________ on the highways.	☐
Wenn du in den USA Eier bestellst, fragt der Kellner, ob du sie als Spiegelei oder beidseitig gebraten möchtest.	When you order eggs in the US, the waiter will ask if you want them ____________ or ____________.	☐ ☐
Unser neuer Geschichtslehrer ist toll. Hast du übrigens schon deine Geschichtshausaufgaben gemacht?	Our new History teacher is great. ____________, have you done your History homework yet?	☐
Auf langen Reisen ist mir ein bequemer Sitzplatz wichtig.	On long journeys a ____________ seat is important to me.	☐

9 Odd man out

Which word doesn't fit? Underline it.

1. breakfast – sunny side up – dinner – lunch
2. tasty – comfortable – fabulous – stranded
3. delayed – on Thursday – in March – at 8 a.m.
4. highway – exit – Interstate – arrow
5. over easy – pancake – sunny side up – pastrami
6. holiday – work – vacation – break
7. by the way – chaos – problem – breakdown
8. hotline – sacred – stranded – rescue

→ GK pages 62/63
→ EK pages 66/67

What do you remember?

Meine Eltern schicken mich jedes Jahr in ein Sommerlager.	My parents send me to summer ______________ every year.	☐
Hast du jemals Skifahren ausprobiert? 	Have you ever tried ____________________?	☐
Wenn du eine Party machst, solltest du zunächst Einladungen versenden. Zweitens musst du genügend Essen und Getränke kaufen.	When you have a party, you should ____________________ send invitations. ____________________, you have to buy enough food and drinks.	☐ ☐
Welche Art von Handy hast du?	What __________________ of cell phone do you have?	☐
Bist du glücklich mit deinem Ergebnis im Englischtest?	Are you happy with your ________________________ in the English test?	☐
Die Putzkraft in der Schule heißt John.	The _______________________ at school is called John.	☐

10 Word grid

Put the words from the grid above in the right place in the grid below. Then use the letters in the marked boxes to fill in the word below.

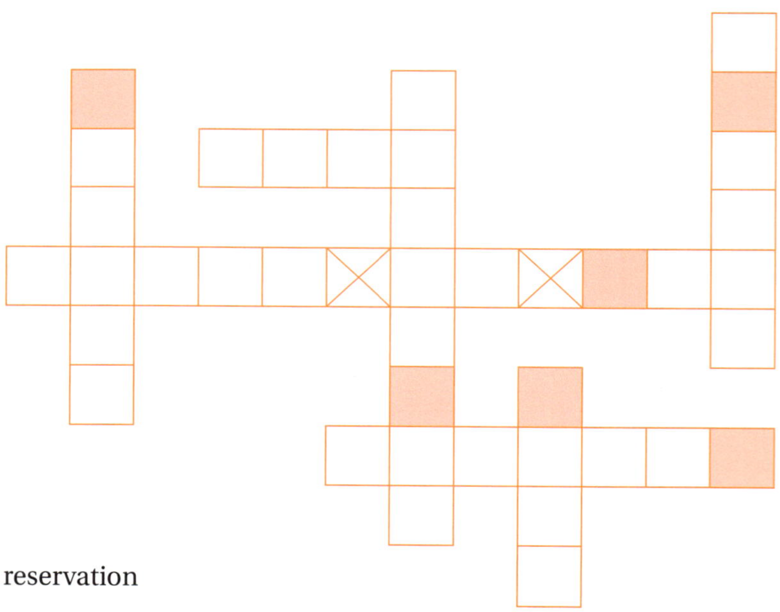

For some American tribes this reservation is a ___ ___ ___ ___ ___ ___ place.

→ EK pages 60/66

What do you remember?	
Der Kofferraum eines Autos ist für Taschen und Gepäck.	The ________________ of a car is for bags and luggage.
Vor einer Stunde gab es einen Unfall auf der Autobahn. Die beiden Autos stehen immer noch am Straßenrand.	An hour ago there was an accident on the ________________. The two cars are still on the ________________________.
Den ganzen Winter war der See gefroren, aber jetzt beginnt er aufzutauen.	All winter the lake was ________________, but now it is starting to ________________.
Mein Bruder ist Kellner und bedient in einem sehr teuren Restaurant.	My brother is a waiter and ________________ in a very expensive restaurant.
Der Grand Canyon ist riesig. Er ist eine überwältigende Sehenswürdigkeit.	The Grand Canyon is ________________. It's an ____________________ sight.
Oft findet man Wasser im unteren Teil einer Schlucht.	You often find water at the bottom of a ________________.
Als meine amerikanische Freundin einen schlimmen Fahrradunfall hatte, rief sie ganz laut „Mama!"	When my American friend had a bad accident with her bike, she was shouting "______________!" quite loudly.
Was sind zehn Prozent von 45?	What is ten ____________________ of 45?

11 Rhyming words

Find a word that rhymes from the grid above.

1. four ________________
2. last ________________
3. curves ________________
4. punk ________________

12 What can you say?

Match the two parts of the sentences correctly.

1. Thirty-six per cent of people in New York
2. We waited on the roadside
3. When an American is talking about the Interstate
4. The Grand Canyon is overwhelming
5. It was so cold on Tuesday
6. A very attractive man

a. that the trunk was frozen closed!
b. because it is so vast.
c. were born abroad.
d. he means the motorway.
e. served my mom at the diner.
f. and looked at the gorge until rescue arrived.

→ GK pages 64/65
→ EK pages 68/69

What do you remember?

Wir müssen uns morgen um 8 Uhr auf den Weg machen.	We need to ______ at 8 a.m. tomorrow.	☐
Pass bitte auf, wenn du die Straße überquerst!	Please take care when you ______ the street.	☐
Es ist ein Abenteuer, im Auto herumzureisen. Du weißt nie, wo du landen wirst.	It's an adventure to ______ in the car. You never know where you'll ______.	☐ ☐
Lasst uns einfach fahren, bis wir einen Ort finden, der uns gefällt.	Let's just drive ______ we find a place that we like.	☐
Deutschland teilt mit neun anderen Ländern die Grenzen.	Germany shares ______ with nine other countries.	☐
Dieser neue Laden verkauft tolles Zeug. Ich könnte dort sogar etwas für Kim finden.	That new shop sells great ______. I ______ even find something for Kim there.	☐ ☐
Wie lange dauert dieses Lied?	How long does this song ______?	☐
Dieser Barmann ist Mexikaner. Er ist letztes Jahr in die USA gekommen.	That ______ is ______. He came to the US last year.	☐ ☐
Das Foto auf deinem Führerschein sieht lustig aus.	The photo on your ______ looks funny.	☐
Du könntest deine Haare für die Party mit einer anderen Farbe besprühen!	You could ______ your hair a different colour for the party!	☐

13 Find the mistakes

Find two mistakes in each sentence and correct them.

1. The barmann mite make you a milkshake. ______ ______
2. Can I cross boarders with this driver's laicense? ______ ______
3. My Mexikan friend sprayd her new bike red. ______ ______
4. We ennded up at a lonely rost area. ______ ______
5. I love to set on and to go plaices. ______ ______
6. My mom hates choas and stoof like that. ______ ______
7. First if all, the two barmans at my boss' big party were awful. ______ ______
8. And secondli, the band only played til 10 p.m.! ______ ______
9. Why does this traffic jam lask so long? We're nearly at our exet! ______ ______
10. We krossed the canjon on a tiny bridge – that was exciting! ______ ______

→ GK pages 64/65
→ EK pages 68/69

What do you remember?	
Hattest du Heimweh, als du in Wales gelebt hast?	Did you ______ when you lived in Wales?
Bären können meilenweit riechen, deshalb muss man beim Camping sorgfältig mit Essen umgehen.	______ can smell ______, so you have to be careful with food when you're camping.
Im Herbst kann man Arbeit als Obstpflücker finden.	In the autumn you can find work as a fruit ______.
Endlich hat José mit Leroy Freundschaft geschlossen.	José has finally ______ with Leroy.
Hispano-Amerikaner können normalerweise Spanisch und Englisch sprechen.	______ can usually speak ______ and English.
Ich verstehe die Englisch-Hausaufgabe nicht ganz, aber ich werde sie irgendwie machen.	I don't fully understand the English homework, but ______ I will do it.
Das Museum zieht jeden Tag mehr als 300 Besucher an.	The museum ______ more than 300 visitors every day.
Brauchst du morgen eine Mitfahrgelegenheit in die Schule?	Do you need a ______ to school tomorrow?
Hast du zu Hause Zugang zum Internet?	Do you have ______ to the Internet at home?
Niemand weiß, wann eine Razzia stattfinden wird.	No one knows when a ______ will take place.
Wir gehen morgen einkaufen, in Ordnung?	We'll go shopping tomorrow, ______?

14 Letter puzzle

Find the correct words and put them into the grid.

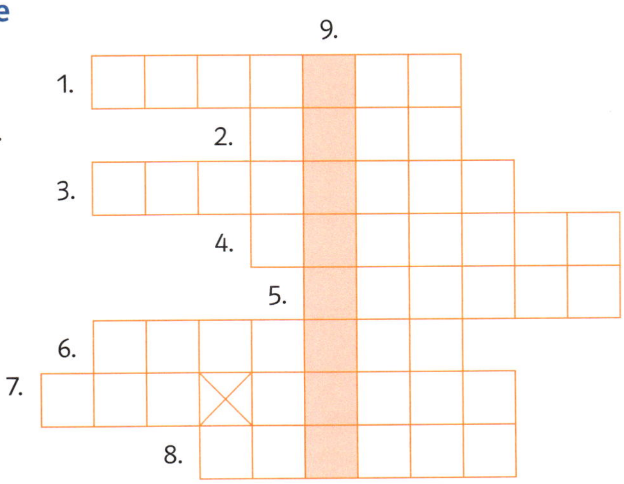

1. It's crazy – … she always wins!
2. My car is broken, but luckily I got a … to work today.
3. I felt … at the camp.
4. Something from Spain is …
5. Do you have Internet … ?
6. On holiday we made … with two English boys.
7. … means the same as *OK*.
8. A person who picks something is a …
9. Many people from Mexico live here – it's an … neighborhood.

→ EK pages 67/72

What do you remember?	
Könntest du mir bitte sagen, wo die Toilette ist?	Could you tell me where the ______________ is, please?
Wenn ich zur Arbeit in den Supermarkt gehe, benutze ich den Eingang für das Personal.	When I go to work at the supermarket, I use the ______________ for the ______________.
Im Urlaub hatte ich ein ganz schön verrücktes Erlebnis …	On holiday I had a __________ crazy ______________.
Glaubst du, dass ich im Casino Glück haben werde?	Do you think I will __________________ at the casino?
Das war knapp! Ich habe dich gewarnt, dass das Wasser heiß ist!	______________________! I ______________ you that the water is hot!
Du darfst im Klassenzimmer nicht Skateboard fahren.	You __________ not ______________ to ride a skateboard in the classroom.
Es ist kalt draußen, aber ich spiele auf jeden Fall Fußball. 	It's cold outside, but I'll play football ______________.
Wenn du diesen Test wieder nicht bestehst, wirst du bestraft!	If you don't pass this test again, you'll ______________!
Fummle nicht die ganze Zeit an deinen Haaren herum – das macht mich nervös!	Don't ______________ with your hair all the time – you're making me nervous!
Der Lehrer klebte die Arbeit der Klasse an die Wand.	The teacher ______________ the class' work on the wall.
Neben dem Freizeitpark gibt es einen riesigen Parkplatz.	Next to the theme park there is a huge ____________________.

15 Questions and answers

Match the questions with the correct answers.

1. Did you warn her about the dangerous dog?
2. Am I allowed to use the restroom?
3. Are you waiting in the parking lot?
4. How was your Spanish lesson?
5. It was pretty cool, wasn't it?
6. You really got it at school today. Why?
7. Will you make lots of new friends at camp?

a. No. I'm at the entrance.
b. Cool? It was an overwhelming experience!
c. No way! And I'll feel homesick anyway.
d. Well, I stuck maple syrup to the teacher's chair …
e. Awful. I just fiddled with my pen.
f. No, but she got lucky. It was asleep!
g. No. It's only for staff.

What do you remember?		
Von welchem Bahnsteig fährt der Zug nach Boston ab?	From which ____________ does the train to Boston leave?	☐
Der Mechaniker, der mein Auto reparierte, war sehr nett.	The ____________ who fixed my car was very friendly.	☐
Ein Baum steht in der Mitte des Gartens.	There is a tree in the ____________ of the garden.	☐
Nirgendwo kann man besser leben als hier!	____________ is better to live than here!	☐
Beschreibe bitte die Typen auf Sandys Party.	Please ____________ the blokes at Sandy's party.	☐
Kannst du das laute Bellen nebenan hören?	Can you hear the loud ____________ next door?	☐
Du kannst Oma nicht besuchen, während sie so krank ist.	You can't visit Grandma ____________ she's so ill.	☐
Nur die Hälfte der Klasse fährt auf Klassenfahrt nach London.	Only ____________ the class are going on a school trip to London.	☐
Christopher Columbus entdeckte Amerika.	Christopher Columbus ____________ America.	☐

16 Word search

Look for the nine words from the grid above. You can find them across → and down ↓.

P	C	K	N	N	S	A	E	T	O	I	H
O	Q	N	W	W	T	N	M	S	H	K	A
P	E	D	E	S	C	R	I	B	E	C	L
R	S	T	T	I	W	F	D	A	L	M	F
S	F	M	P	M	Y	W	D	R	M	E	K
O	E	T	O	U	C	S	L	K	I	C	Y
R	N	O	W	H	E	R	E	I	A	H	W
G	N	M	H	B	G	W	K	N	E	A	L
I	A	N	I	O	G	E	S	G	A	N	T
E	I	P	L	A	T	F	O	R	M	I	B
S	O	G	E	H	E	A	E	I	N	C	D
D	I	S	C	O	V	E	R	E	D	T	R

Revision

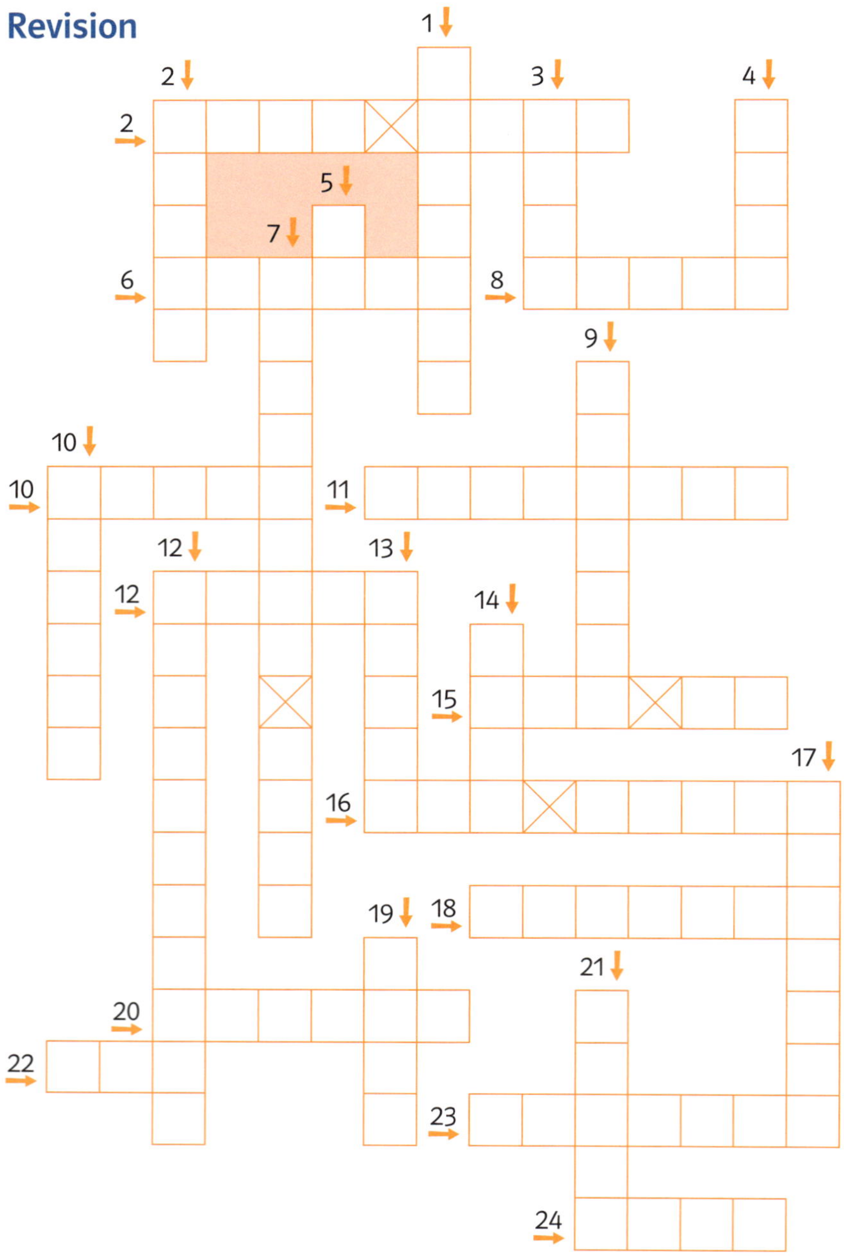

Down

1. There are lots of … in Las Vegas.
2. Cowboys work here.
3. door for leaving a building
4. Did you … new friends in Chicago?
5. … the way, do you also like skiing?
7. You can see animals, plants and great scenery in a …
9. not on time
10. What was the … of the vote? – We lost.
12. If you go for a walk in the reservation, wear … shoes!
13. things
14. 
17. Look at this huge canyon! And at those tall trees! What an awesome …!
19. At summer … you live in a tent.
21. The Statue of Liberty is a famous … in New York.

Across

2. Let's stop at the highway … for a break.
6. The Grand … is in Arizona.
8. A Native American … lives on the reservation.
10. The best cowboys are trying to win this.
11. fantastic, awesome
12. When there's no order, there's …
15. I'll start my trip in New York and … in Los Angeles.
16. We crossed the whole state, so we drove … and miles and miles!
18. This is a driver's … 

20. His job is to make drinks. 
22. First of … , you pay. Secondly, you sit back and enjoy.
23. important main road
24. Carrots are a … of vegetable.

→ GK pages 72/73
→ EK pages 76/77

What do you remember?

Der Oscar ist ein Preis für Schauspieler und sieht wie ein kleines Standbild aus. 	The Oscar is an ______________ for actors and looks like a small ______________.
Hast du Jesse Raymonds neues Album gehört? Er ist ein toller R&B Sänger.	Have you heard Jesse Raymond's new ______________? He's a great ______________ singer.
Ich möchte gern ein rückenfreies Kleid zu dem Tanz tragen. Oder findest du das zu gewagt?	I'd like to wear a ______________ dress to the dance. Or do you think it's too ______________?
Mein Abendkleid ist von einer coolen jungen Designerin. 	My ______________ is from a cool young ______________.
Die meisten Leute tanzen gern zu Latinomusik.	Most people like to dance to ______________.
Die Schauspielerin trägt ein rotes Kleid, das tief ausgeschnitten und sehr glamourös ist.	The actress is wearing a red dress, which is ______________ and very ______________.
Hast du die Theaterproduktion gestern Abend genossen?	Did you enjoy the theater ______________ last night?

1 What can you say?

Match the two parts of the sentences.

1. The new album of my favourite band
2. I'd like to wear the low-cut evening dress,
3. This action movie won an award
4. This fashion designer is so famous
5. The award-winning R&B singer is glamorous in front of the camera,

a. but my boyfriend likes the backless one better.
b. but in private places she can be outrageous.
c. that there's a statue of him in the trendy harbor area.
d. for best production.
e. has some Latino on it.

2 More letters than you need

You only need every third letter. The words are from the grid above.

1. fndamebssjhiehgbsnwreqar ______________
2. prsibteiabhtnlusfe ______________
3. nmbweahdcljklslytewzsass ______________
4. rtamnwliabhrsfd ______________
5. vboebusrtfdrqsavbgwmejlobvuwzs ______________
6. lkadllmvbnnudnm ______________

→ GK pages 72/73
→ EK pages 76/77

What do you remember?	
Am Ende jedes Schuljahrs gibt es eine Zeremonie. Ein Fotograf wird auch da sein.	At the end of each school year there's a ______________ . A ______________ will be there, too.
Magst du nur Countrymusik?	Do you only like ______________ ?
Die Band meiner Schwester spielt Rockmusik.	My sister's band plays ______________ .
Der Spitzname von Charlotte ist Lotti.	Charlotte's ______________ is Lotti.
Wer wird den Preis für den besten Film verleihen?	Who will ______________ the award for Best ______________ ?
Ich glaube, Bob Marley war der erste große Star des Reggae.	I think Bob Marley was the first big star of ______________ .
Der Teppichboden in meinem Schlafzimmer ist grün.	The ______________ in my bedroom is green.
Deutsche Volksmusik ist echt furchtbar, finde ich.	German ______________ is really horrible, I think.
Viele berühmte Soulmusik-Stars kommen aus den USA.	Many famous ______________ stars come from the US.
Die Leute begannen circa 1980 Dancehall zu hören.	People began to listen to ______________ in about 1980.
Wer ist übrigens dein Lieblingsstar bei Popmusik?	By the way, who is your favourite star in ______________ ?

3 The correct word

Underline the correct word to complete the sentences.

1. In 2001 *A Beautiful Mind* won the Oscar for Best *(Photo/Cinema/Picture)*.
2. A *(picker/photographer/photo)* took pictures at the award ceremony.
3. Country sounds like a kind of *(folk/folks/fork)*.
4. There are many large *(rocks/pops/souls)* at the Grand Canyon.
5. – She's called Helen, but her *(funny name/nickname/crazy name)* is DH.
6. – Why DH? Because she loves *(dog's house/dancehall/dirty hero)* music?
7. – No, it means 'dearest Helen' because she has such a thoughtful *(seat/sound/soul)*.
8. They presented the reggae award on the red *(bed/carpet/shelf)*.

→ EK pages 76/77

What do you remember?		
Jemand, der für eine Zeitung arbeitet, gehört zur Presse.	Someone who works for a newspaper belongs to the ______________ .	☐
Der Fußballspieler hielt die Trophäe hoch über seinen Kopf.	The football player ______________ the ______________ high above his head.	☐☐
Bist du Mitglied eines Sportvereins?	Are you a ______________ of a sports club?	☐
Darf ich um Ihre Aufmerksamkeit bitten?	May I have your ______________ , please?	☐
Es sind nur noch wenige Läden übrig, die Schallplatten verkaufen.	There are only few shops left that sell ______________ .	☐
Der Preis für das Mittagessen beinhaltet ein Getränk.	The price for lunch ______________ a drink.	☐
Ich nahm an einem Rennen in meiner Alterskategorie teil.	I took part in a race in my age ______________ .	☐

4 Life in a pop group

Put in the correct words from the grid above.

Jamie is a ______________ of a famous pop group, but he doesn't always like his job.

The band has just won the 'Best Rock Song' award for its brand new ______________.

"Well, our music ______________ reggae, soul and dancehall. But definitely no rock!

So we don't belong to that ______________ at all," Jamie tells his girlfriend. "Instead of this one I really want the 'Best R&B Song' award."

Everywhere he goes Jamie also gets a lot of ______________ from teenage girls and from members of the ______________. He hates it.

Finally his girlfriend picks up his award and ______________ it. "I'm so proud of you, Jamie!" she whispers. "Oh, it's just a stupid ______________," he answers. "Only jerks care about things like that!"

5 Phonetics

Read the words. Then write them down correctly.

1. [ɪn'klu:d] ______________
2. ['membə] ______________
3. [pres] ______________
4. ['trəʊfi] ______________
5. [ə'tentʃn] ______________
6. ['kætəgri] ______________

→ GK page 74
→ EK page 78

What do you remember?

Eine Kamera<u>blende</u> bewegt sich sehr schnell.	A camera ____________ moves very quickly.	☐
Mein Bruder <u>gründet</u> gerade eine neue Band.	My brother is just ____________ a new band.	☐
Um ein Paket zu packen, braucht man dickes Papier, <u>Schnur</u> und eine Schachtel.	To pack a packet you need thick paper, ____________ and a box.	☐
Der Schauspieler machte eine <u>Bewegung</u> mit seiner Hand.	The actor made a ____________ with his hand.	☐
Für die ersten Filme brauchte man viele <u>Standfotos</u>.	For the first movies they needed many ____________ .	☐
Niemand erwartete den <u>Aufstieg</u> dieser neuen Band.	No one expected the ____________ of that new band.	☐
Die Leute waren aufgeregt, als sie den ersten <u>Tonfilm</u> sahen.	People were excited when they saw the first ____________ .	☐

6 Letter puzzle

Put the German words into English.

1. Designer
2. Standbild
3. Aufstieg
4. Tonfilm
5. Album
6. einrichten
7. Bewegung
8. Teppichboden
9. Verschluss
10. Seele
11. Schnur
12. rückenfrei

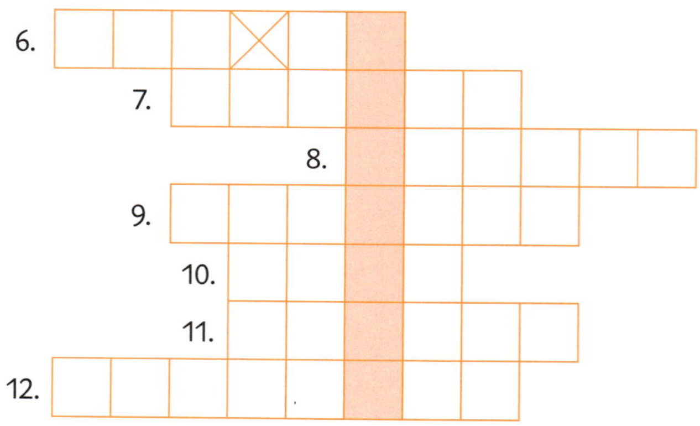

7 Definition

Tick the right definition for each word.

1. talkie
   - ☐ a. a chat
   - ☐ b. a talk show
   - ☐ c. a movie with sound
2. rise
   - ☐ a. a new technology
   - ☐ b. a journey to the top
   - ☐ c. a type of sound
3. motion
   - ☐ a. when something moves
   - ☐ b. when something disappears
   - ☐ c. when something goes down
4. still
   - ☐ a. a photo
   - ☐ b. a film
   - ☐ c. a comic

→ EK pages 78/79

What do you remember?

In unserem Badezimmer gibt es zwei Schränke.	In our bathroom there are two ______ .	☐
Als Erwachsene würde ich gerne ein Buch veröffentlichen. 	As an adult I would like to ______ a book.	☐
Hast du meine Geburtstagskarte erhalten?	Did you ______ my birthday card?	☐
Dieses Mathe-Problem ist sehr kompliziert.	This Maths problem is very ______ .	☐
Die Musik für einen Film heißt Partitur.	The music for a film is called a music ______ .	☐
Hört auf, Witze zu machen! Das folgende Thema ist ernst.	Stop joking! The following topic is ______ .	☐
Man kann im Museum eine echte Rakete sehen.	You can see a real ______ in the museum.	☐
In dieser E-Mail habe ich für Sie einige zusätzliche Informationen angehängt.	In this e-mail I have ______ some extra information for you.	☐
Hast du jemals einen Western gesehen?	Have you ever seen a ______ ?	☐

8 Word grid

Put the nine words from the grid above in the correct places below. Then use the letters in the marked boxes to fill in the word below.

The punk band received an award for the loudest

___ ___ ___ ___ ___.

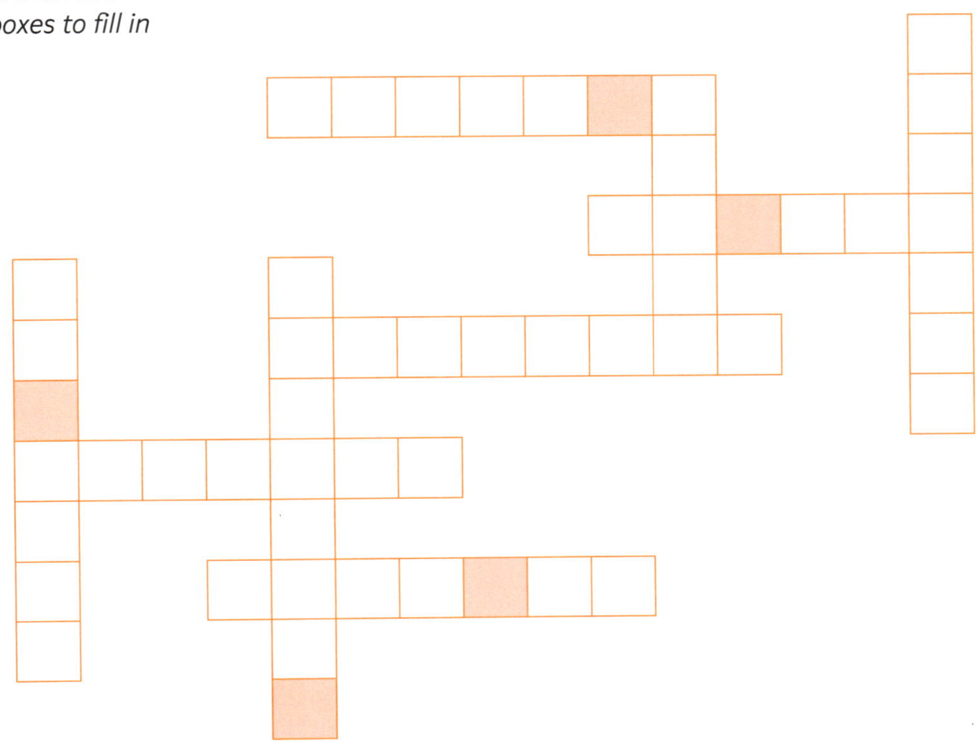

→ GK pages 72/74

What do you remember?		
Alexander Graham Bell war der Erfinder des Telefons.	Alexander Graham Bell was the ______________ of the phone.	☐
Hat ein Stummfilm jemals einen Oscar gewonnen?	Has a ______________ ever won an Oscar?	☐
Wer führte bei diesem Film Regie?	Who ______________ this movie?	☐
Der Schauspieler, der gerade die Bühne betreten hat, sieht sehr nervös aus.	The actor who has just gone on the ______________ looks very nervous.	☐
Die Lehrerin bat ihre Klasse, während der Klassenarbeit leise zu sein.	The teacher asked her class to be ______________ during the test.	☐
Dieses alte Auto hat einen schrecklich lauten Motor.	That old car has a terribly loud ______________ .	☐
Als Model ist es dein Job, für Fotos zu posieren.	As a model it's your job to ______________ for photos.	☐
Diese Fabrik stellt Autos her.	This factory ______________ cars.	☐
Meine Mutter machte einen Kuchen, der die Form eines Flugzeugs hatte.	My mother made a cake which was the ______________ of a plane.	☐

9 Questions and answers

Match the questions with the correct answers.

1. Why is the motor silent?
2. Did Tim Burton produce *Alice in Wonderland*?
3. What shape is the stage?
4. A girl is posing for the photographers. Who is she?
5. Who was Thomas Edison?
6. Can you set up the camera, please?

a. She's in a new silent movie.
b. It's broken.
c. Yes. I'll open the shutter.
d. No, he directed it.
e. It's a circle.
f. He was an inventor.

10 Phonetics

Read the words. Then write them down correctly.

1. [steɪdʒ] ______________
2. [dɪ'rekt] ______________
3. [pəʊz] ______________
4. ['saɪlənt] ______________
5. ['məʊtə] ______________
6. [ɪn'ventə] ______________

→ GK pages 76/77
→ EK pages 80/81

What do you remember?

Ich mag es, mich am Wochenende mit meinen Freunden zu entspannen.	I like to ____________ with my friends at the weekend.
Meine Gitarrestunden sind echt langweilig. Wenn ich mit Freunden improvisiere, habe ich viel mehr Spaß. 	My ____________ lessons are really boring. When I ____________ with friends, I have much more fun.
Wenn er die Klunker trägt, sieht James aus wie ein Gangster.	When he wears the ____________ , James looks like a real ____________ !
Wenn du eine Nachricht in einem Internetforum posten möchtest, musst du dich zuerst anmelden.	If you want to ____________ a message in an Internet ____________, you must ____________ first.
Meine besten Freunde sind für mich wirklich von Bedeutung.	My best friends really ____________ to me.
Dieser Chatroom ist für Leute, die Popmusik mögen. Es ist kostenlos, alle Nachrichten anzuschauen.	This ____________ is for people who like pop music. You can ____________ all messages for free.
Ein Radio-DJ hat in seiner Sendung meinen Lieblingsrapper beleidigt.	A radio DJ ____________ my favourite ____________ on his show.
Wir müssen heute über diese wichtige Angelegenheit sprechen.	We must talk about this important ____________ today.

11 Word search

Look for the words from the grid above. You can find them across → and down ↓

D	F	T	R	A	B	M	R	O	M	D	R	H
I	P	Y	S	F	R	E	E	S	T	Y	L	E
S	O	D	L	A	U	H	G	T	E	R	Y	I
S	S	O	B	F	C	H	I	L	L	O	U	T
E	T	B	L	R	C	D	S	T	Y	U	R	A
D	E	A	I	W	H	F	T	S	V	I	E	W
W	S	D	N	Q	A	H	E	I	N	M	D	S
G	A	N	G	S	T	E	R	N	R	A	A	R
G	Y	M	B	U	R	X	B	A	A	B	E	F
H	D	R	L	I	O	Y	N	E	P	V	R	O
A	I	E	I	I	O	Y	I	W	P	V	T	R
P	M	V	N	L	M	A	T	T	E	R	G	U
P	S	O	G	U	I	T	A	R	R	E	E	M

→ GK pages 76/77
→ EK pages 80/81

What do you remember?		
Warum bildet ihr nicht eine Band? Das würde doch Spaß machen.	Why don't you ______ a band? That would be fun.	☐
Lasst uns den neuen Freizeitpark ansehen!	Let's ______ the new theme park!	☐
Das ist mein letztes Angebot – komm, 20 Dollar für fünf CDs ist nicht viel!	This is my last ______ – come on, 20 dollars for five CDs isn't a lot!	☐
Ich wohne in einem Vorort von Frankfurt.	I live in a ______ of Frankfurt.	☐
Meine Lieblingsindieband wird bald hier auftreten und ich möchte mit drei Kumpels hingehen.	My favourite ______ band will soon perform here and I want to go there with three ______ .	☐ ☐
Der attraktivste Musiker in meiner Lieblingsband ist der Schlagzeuger. 	The most attractive ______ in my favourite band is the ______ .	☐ ☐
Ich mag alle Schulfächer außer Mathematik.	I like all school subjects, ______ Maths.	☐
Ich mag Hip-Hop, aber manche Lieder sind voller Verachtung. Das stört mich ziemlich.	I like hip hop, but some songs are full of ______ . That bothers me a lot.	☐
Kannst du mir oft eine E-Mail schreiben, während ich im Krankenhaus bin?	Can you ______ me often while I'm in the hospital?	☐
Jetzt hören meine Eltern am liebsten Funk.	Now my parents like listening to ______ best.	☐
Aber mein Vater spielte einmal Bass in einer Metalband!	But my father once played ______ in a ______ band!	☐ ☐

12 Find the mistakes

Find two mistakes in each sentence and correct the words.

1. The drammer comes from a suberb of Chicago. ______ ______
2. My friends want to check in a new funck club. ______ ______
3. I play guitar and my homy plays base. ______ ______
4. You should buy this rekord today. There's a special over. ______ ______
5. An electric gitar has many metall parts. ______ ______
6. The indee drummer showed the R&B singer disrespekt. ______ ______
7. Yesterday I i-mailed everyone, eccept the rapper. ______ ______
8. Four musicions decided that they wanted to farm a band. ______ ______

→ GK page 76

What do you remember?		
Der Musikstil, den ich am wenigsten mag, ist Heavy Metal.	The style of music that I like ______ is ______ .	☐ ☐
Manchmal höre ich auch Alternative.	Sometimes I also listen to ______ .	☐
Wo die Anfänge der Punkmusik liegen, darüber wird immer noch gestritten.	People are still arguing about where ______ really started.	☐
Das kleinste Schwimmbecken ist nur für kleine Kinder.	The smallest swimming pool is ______ for young children.	☐
Kennst du jemanden, der an Countrymusik interessiert ist?	Do you know anybody who ______ country?	☐
Meine Freundin möchte eine Independentband an unserer Schule gründen.	My girlfriend wants to set up an ______ band at our school.	☐

13 At the record shop

Put in the correct words from the grid above.

The two friends José and Kingsley are at their local record shop.

"Can I help you," asks the shop assistant.

"José _ _ _ _ _ _ R&B, but I like metal most of all – sometimes even _ _ _ _ _ _ _ _ _ _," says Kingsley.

"All right," says the assistant. "If you like heavy metal, you probably like _ _ _ _, too. Or you might like the Black Statues. They're a brand new _ _ _ _ _ _ _ _ _ _ _ band from Miami."

"I'm not so sure. You know, really I'm _ _ _ _ _ _ _ _ into metal," says Kingsley.

"And what about indie?" the assistant says.

"What is indie?" asks Kingsley.

"It's short for _ _ _ _ _ _ _ _ _ _ _," explains José. "I don't like it. In fact, it's my _ _ _ _ _ favourite music."

"Well, then I'll probably like it a lot!" laughs Kingsley. "Although we're friends, we like very different types of music. OK, which good indie band can I listen to, please?"

→ GK pages 78/80
→ GK pages 82/84

What do you remember?

Auf dieser Prachtstraße sieht man öfter Limousinen.	On this ______________ you often see ________________ .
Dan borgte fünf Euro, weil er pleite ist.	Dan borrowed five euros because he is ____________ .
Jede Autobahn hat mindestens zwei Fahrspuren.	Every Interstate has at least two ________________ .
Hey, warum lässt du den Champagner nicht knallen?	Hey, why don't you _________ the ________________ ?
Du brauchst Licht, um deinen Schatten zu sehen.	You need light to see your ________________ .
Der Vogel landete am Rand des Daches.	The bird landed on the ___________ of the roof.
Die Ärztin suchte nach Lebenszeichen ihres Patienten.	The doctor looked for her patient's ____________________ .
Unsere Nachbarn sind echt unfreundlich.	Our neighbours are really __________________ .
Es ist nicht immer höflich, das Wort „Hintern" zu benutzen.	It isn't always polite to use the word '_____________'.
Kennst du alle Wörter des Refrains?	Do you know all the words of the _________________ ?
Unsere Klasse braucht Begleitpersonen für die nächste Klassenfahrt.	Our class needs _______________ for the next class trip.
Wasser ist für das Überleben unerlässlich.	Water is ___________ for survival.
Das Badezimmer ist makellos! Hast du es geputzt?	The bathroom is _______________! Have you cleaned it?

14 Which word it is?

Choose the right word and complete the sentences.

1. Your _____________ is longest in the early evening.

2. The girls are going to homecoming in a _______________ .

3. My house is in a tiny little _____________ .

4. Steve can't buy champagne for his birthday party because he's _________ .

→ GK page 80
→ EK page 84

What do you remember?

Ich habe keine Ahnung, wo man in dieser Stadt Kaviar kaufen kann.	I ______ where you can buy ______ in this city.
Getränke mit Alkohol kann ich nur schlürfen!	I can only ______ drinks with alcohol!
Unterstützen deine Eltern dich und deine Lebensart?	Do your parents ______ you and your ______?
Trina verdient es wirklich, in diesem Jahr Ballkönigin zu werden.	Trina really ______ to be homecoming queen this year.
Ich schwelge in Erinnerungen an meinen ersten Freund …	I'm ______ about my first boyfriend …
Die Frau schaukelte ihre kleine Tochter.	The woman ______ her little ______.
Als ich den Kampf sah, konnte ich nichts tun außer schreien und wegrennen. Dennoch rief ich Minuten später die Polizei an.	When I first saw the fight, I couldn't do anything ______ shout and run away. ______, after a few minutes I called the police.
Kopfsalat kocht man nicht; man isst ihn roh.	You don't cook lettuce; you eat it ______.
Egal wie oft ich Skifahren gehe, ich habe immer noch Angst vor diesem verdammten Sport!	______ how often I go skiing, I'm still frightened of that ______ sport!
Gibt es hier in der Nähe eine Bank?	Is there a ______ near here?

15 Rhyming words

Find a word from the grid above that rhymes with a word below.

1. water ______
2. curves ______
3. floor ______
4. thank ______
5. ham ______
6. slow ______

16 Odd man out

Which word or phrase doesn't fit? Underline it.

1. I have no idea. – I don't know. – I'm sure. – I have no clue.
2. to sip – to rock – to eat – to drink
3. to destroy – to look after – to support – to help
4. caviar – lifestyle – champagne – bagel

→ EK pages 80/87

What do you remember?	
Es ist echt peinlich, wenn mein Vater Slang benutzt.	It's really embarrassing when my dad uses ____________ .
Helen wird sich nach der Schule bei mir melden.	Helen will ____________ me after school.
Wir sind im selben Team, also will ich nicht gegen dich kämpfen.	We're on the same team, so I don't want to ____________ against you.
Als das Auswahlverfahren begann, schlug ihr Herz immer schneller.	When the tryout started, her ____________ ____________ faster and faster.
Könnten Sie mir einige nützliche Redewendungen für meinen Urlaub beibringen?	Could you teach me some useful ____________ for my holiday?
In welchem Zusammenhang wird das neue Wort hier benutzt?	In which ____________ is the new word used here?
Easy ist ein Synonym für *simple*.	'Easy' is a ____________ for 'simple'.
Wie wäre es heute Abend mit einer Jamsession?	What about a ____________ tonight?
Zum Geburtstag möchte mein Opa einen Satz Briefmarken, die die Schauplätze vergangener Schlachten zeigen.	For his birthday my grandad wants a ____________ of stamps which show the scenes of past ____________ .
Diese Band weiß, wie man seine Fans unterhält.	This band knows how to ____________ their fans.
Meinst du, ich könnte als Freiwillige im Krankhaus arbeiten? Ich möchte es wenigstens ein paar Wochen lang versuchen.	Do you think I could work at the hospital as a ____________ ? At least I'd like to ____________ for a few weeks.
Warum trittst du nicht dem neuen Sportverein bei?	Why don't you ____________ the new sports club?

17 Missing letters

Add the letters to complete the words from the grid.

1. _ _ l _ _ _ _ _ e _
2. _ _ t _ _ _ _ t _
3. b _ _ _ _ _
4. _ _ n _ _ _ _
5. _ _ _ e _ _ _ _ o
6. _ e _ _
7. j _ _
8. _ _ t _ _ _ _ i _
9. _ h _ _ _ _ _
10. _ _ t

→ GK pages 78/81

What do you remember?

Ich liebe den Refrain dieses Lieds, obwohl ich keine seiner vielen Strophen singen kann.	I love the __________ of that song, although I can't sing any of its many __________ .
Wovon hast du letzte Nacht geträumt? 	What did you __________ about last night?
Wenn ein Lied auf der Tanzfläche gut funktioniert, dann ist mir der Liedtext egal.	If a song works well on the dance floor, then I don't care about the __________ .
Der junge Schauspieler hatte Angst vor der letzten Szene, weil er darin eine berühmte Schauspielerin küssen musste.	The young actor was nervous about the final __________ because in it he had to kiss a famous actress.
Dein Bruder ist ein ziemlich cooler Typ.	Your brother is a pretty cool __________ .
Es war die Hölle, als ich mir das Bein brach und drei Monate lang nicht Fußball spielen konnte!	It was __________ when I broke my leg and couldn't play football for three months!
Viele Maschinen machen das Leben der Menschen einfacher.	Many __________ make people's lives easier.
Mein Lieblingslied ist von einem amerikanischen Rapper.	My favourite song is __________ an American rapper.

18 What's the word?

Read the definition and write down the correct word.

1. It does a lot of work, so humans needn't do it: __________
2. You sing this part of a song again and again: __________
3. The words in a song: __________
4. The opposite of paradise: __________
5. During your sleep you might do this in your head: __________
6. You can call a man this: __________
7. This is a part of a play: __________
8. This is part of a song as well as part of a poem: __________

Revision

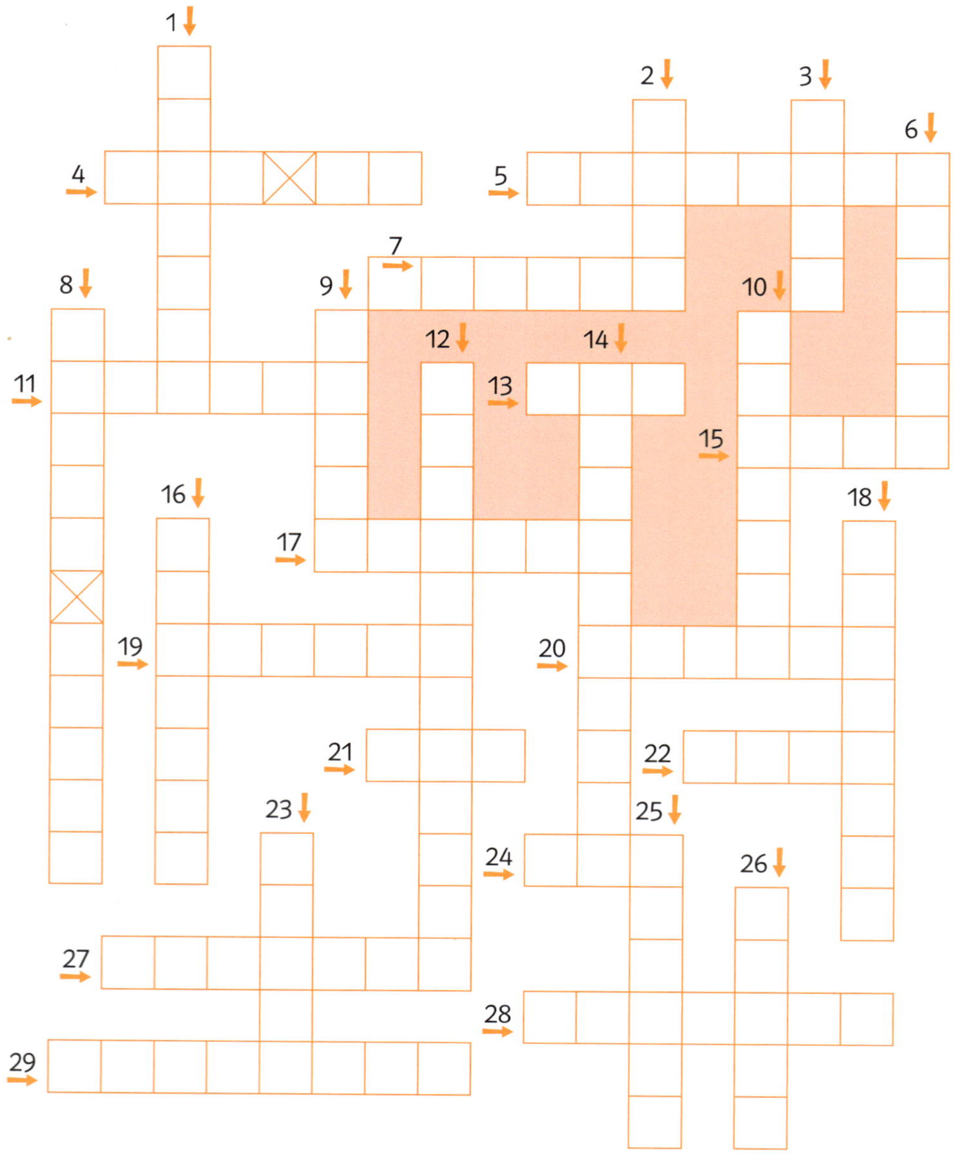

Across

4. einrichten
5. makellos
7. Refrain
11. Latinomusik
13. Popmusik
15. abschicken
17. ausmachen
19. Schnur
20. Gitarre
21. roh
22. bilden
24. Hintern
27. Schlagzeuger/Schlagzeugerin
28. Verschluss
29. Anstandswauwau

Down

1. präsentieren
2. beleidigen
3. Aufstieg
6. außer
8. Klunker
9. Forum
10. unterstützen
12. Fotograf/Fotografin
14. ausgefallen
16. verdienen
18. Zeremonie
23. Kumpel
25. Vorort
26. lebenswichtig

Lösungen

Unit 1

What do you remember?

background, skyscraper, foreground, symbol, freedom, steps, harbor, jogger, borough, kickboard, public, immigrants, neighborhoods, theater, neon

1 Definition

1. c, 2. a, 3. b, 4. a, 5. b, 6. c

What do you remember?

Immigration, war, Dutch, founded, English, named, Irish, famine, quota

2 Find the mistakes

1. famine 2. Irish 3. Dutch 4. freedom 5. wars 6. quotas 7. English 8. name 9. immigration 10. skyscraper 11. borough 12. steps

What do you remember?

seasick, official, Belgian, run out, emigrate, native Americans, poverty, native, Oppression

3 Questions and answers

1. c, 2. e, 3. a, 4. b, 5. d

4 Letter puzzle

					O	F	F	I	C	I	A	L
					N	A	T	I	V	E		
					E	M	I	G	R	A	T	E
		E	N	G	L	I	S	H				
B	E	L	G	I	A	N						
					S	E	A	S	I	C	K	

What do you remember?

ball, yarn, unwinds, thread, hub, farther and farther, hope, little, farther, coffee, opinion

5 Phonetics

1. coffee 2. little 3. hub 4. hope 5. ball 6. thread 7. opinion 8. unwind 9. unwound 10. yarn 11. farther; father 12. seasick

6 More letters than you need

1. yarn 2. unwind 3. hope 4. farther 5. hub 6. coffee 7. thread 8. little

What do you remember?

vacation, deli, bagels, dollars, special, cream cheese, cherry, French fries, strawberry, cents, nickel, monster, tip, quarters, cupcake, free

7 Which word is it?

1. monster 2. dollar 3. cherry 4. vacation 5. quarter; nickel 6. French fries 7. free

What do you remember?

Danish, to go, toast, pancakes, maple syrup, cream, bacon, slice, put in, dime, milkshake, turkey, pastrami

8 Word search

T	R	B	A	C	O	N	O	O	B	D	X
O	A	S	P	V	B	Z	X	R	A	I	I
D	A	N	T	F	L	T	E	A	G	N	O
C	U	P	C	A	K	E	A	C	E	P	T
C	R	A	Y	P	E	S	Y	R	L	A	E
W	C	R	E	A	M	C	H	E	E	S	E
E	L	I	S	N	H	A	Y	A	B	T	Z
S	L	T	E	C	T	A	P	M	V	R	Q
F	A	S	G	A	O	T	B	N	O	A	O
M	A	T	R	K	A	T	O	A	S	M	B
M	A	P	L	E	S	Y	R	U	P	I	U
V	E	R	R	E	T	U	R	K	E	Y	Y

What do you remember?

festival, parade, businesses, decorations, fireworks, go on, friendly, dragon, paper

9 Festival time

festival, fireworks, parade, goes on, friendly, vacation, decorations, paper, business

What do you remember?

population, candy, such as, low, activities, mostly, lower

10 Missing letters

1. activities 2. low 3. mostly 4. candy 5. such as 6. lower 7. population

11 Odd man out

1. under 2. population 3. biggest 4. dragon 5. Ireland 6. pound 7. coffee 8. bed

What do you remember?

roared, flat, take off, snapshot, flashed, pilot, tour, Yeah, very, sit back, cool, pointed to, folks

12 What kind of word?

Verb: roared, take off, flashed, sit back, pointed to
Adjective: flat, cool
Noun: snapshot, pilot, tour, folks
Other: yeah, very

What do you remember?

Fahrenheit, heat, fainted, cop, round, switch off, dizzy, electric, workman, drill, repair, mister

13 Which word is it?

1. cop 2. heat 3. Fahrenheit 4. workman, repair

What do you remember?

instructions, quite, are (you) into, was leaning, apartment, relax, forward, sort, loads of

14 Rhyming words

1. loads 2. lean 3. quite 4. relax 5. sort

15 The same

1. sort 2. apartment 3. to be into 4. loads of

16 Teacher talk

Lean forward and listen to my instructions!
We have got loads of work to do!

What do you remember?

whole, pretty, engine, per cent, below, mark, immigrated, all over, run over, huge, top, beginning, at the front

17 What can you say?

1. e, 2. c, 3. g, 4. a, 5. f, 6. b, 7. d

Revision

→ 1. snapshot 6. native 8. parade 10. immigration 15. neighborhood 17. nickel 18. emigrate 19. cents 20. faint 21. paper 22. friendly

↓ 2. poverty 3. toast 4. war 5. deli 7. tour 9. famine 11. background 12. free 13. workman 14. pilot 15. neon 16. bacon 19. cop

Unit 2

What do you remember?

prize, student, curriculum, high school, rally, cheerleaders, homecoming, tryout, grade, breaking news, theme park, yearbook

1 Mrs O'Brien's school days

high school, yearbook, student, cheerleaders, tryouts, prizes, grade, curriculum, homecoming, breaking news

What do you remember?

pledge, Ballroom dancing, everybody, homecoming queen, dress, captain, supporters, jeans, formal, dancing, pompoms, ballroom, chanted, brand, allegiance

2 More letters than you need

1. formal 2. chant 3. pompom 4. allegiance

3 The correct word

1. queen 2. supporter 3. allegiance 4. Jeans 5. captain

What do you remember?

absence, contacted, alcohol, Luckily, permission, slip, dated, adverts, tobacco, drugs, material, Gangs

4 Crossword

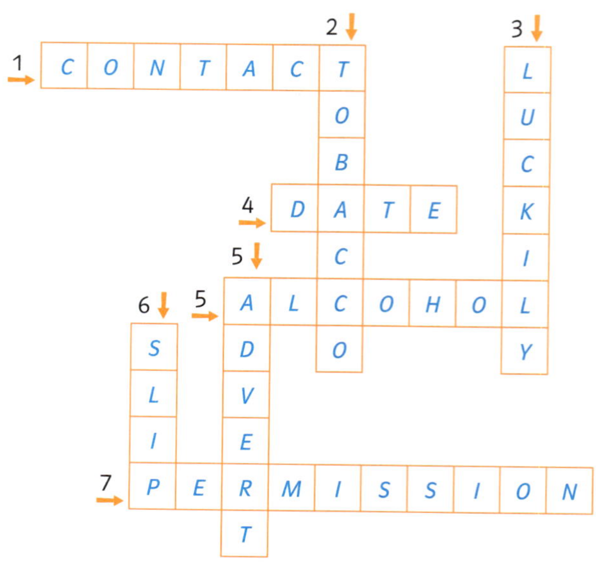

What do you remember?

recess, period, belong to, have a look at, caption, think up, Adults, edit, straight, zone, difference, parent, report, May, absent

5 What can you say?

1. d, 2. a, 3. f, 4. h, 5. g, 6. e, 7. c, 8. b

What do you remember?

date, attractive, movie, still, movies, Hi, there, overdo, thoughtful, end, kiss, move, See you around, jerk, hot, awesome

6 Find the mistakes

1. there, tryout 2. rally, see 3. jerk, tobacco 4. awesome, still 5. date, movies 6. attractive, overdo 7. hot, move 8. ended, kiss

What do you remember?

take care, public schools, pass, elementary school, dare, soccer, upper, less, middle schools

7 Phonetics

1. soccer 2. public school 3. dare 4. pass 5. take care 6. middle school 7. upper 8. elementary school

8 Rhyming words

1. less 2. pass 3. upper 4. care, dare 5. school 6. take

What do you remember?

paid for, juice, rivals, vote, honest, suit, fill, bar, arms

9 Words and pictures

1. bar 2. arms 3. vote for 4. juice 5. suit 6. paid for

What do you remember?

dance floor, front, lie, clumsy, vote, fix, shoulder, mean, Hey, clumsy!

10 Word search

C	R	I	N	Y	T	X	S	D	C	D	I
E	F	R	O	N	T	E	S	T	C	A	I
E	R	H	U	M	E	A	N	S	T	N	A
H	U	O	V	R	Y	I	O	R	D	C	H
E	Y	U	S	U	M	S	E	S	S	E	B
Y	W	C	L	U	M	S	Y	C	A	F	P
H	S	L	I	F	Y	A	A	K	R	L	I
J	S	D	E	L	I	D	E	D	S	O	X
A	V	R	N	V	O	T	Y	E	A	O	Q
C	O	S	H	O	F	I	X	A	T	R	S
Y	T	Z	Y	T	H	O	U	T	D	E	R
G	E	R	S	H	O	U	L	D	E	R	O

What do you remember?

cheerleading, embarrassed, definitely, have graduated, start up, cheer up, hurtful, right, You're kidding, (shopping) mall, latte, kind, Yuk, pose

11 Letter puzzle

					8.							
1.				C	H	E	E	R		U	P	
2.				Y	U	K						
3.		S	T	A	R	T		U	P			
4.	R	I	G	H	T							
5.			D	E	F	I	N	I	T	E	L	Y
6.	G	R	A	D	U	A	T	E				
7.					L	A	T	T	E			

What do you remember?

gossip, guy, training, hanging around, band, awful, wasting, at all, gossip, warm up, stepped, missed

12 Missing letters

1. wasting 2. awful 3. gossip 4. warm up 5. at all 6. missed 7. hanging around 8. training 9. guy 10. band 11. stepped

What do you remember?

cigarette, graduated, university, mistake, ill, at any time, colorful, Survival, period, match, lead, may

13 Questions and answers

1. c, 2. a, 3. e, 4. b, 5. d

14 Odd man out

1. vegetables 2. colorful 3. A-levels 4. cigarette

Revision

→ 3. grade 5. everybody 7. absence 10. juice 11. still 12. advert 13. dare 14. gangs 15. pass 16. lie 19. breaking news 21. vote 22. arm 23. end 24. rally 25. honest

↓ 1. permission 2. soccer 4. elementary school 6. cheerleader 8. ballroom dancing 9. chant 12. awesome 13. date 16. luckily 17. rival 18. dress 20. shoulder

Unit 3

What do you remember?

inventions, robots, space station, astronaut, equipment, space, Earth, outer space, smart, monitor, virtual, pacemaker, reality, tractor, plough

1 Find the words

					E	A	R	T	H			
O	U	T	E	R	X	S	P	A	C	E		
		S	M	A	R	T						
						R	O	B	O	T	S	
					M	O	N	I	T	O	R	
		I	N	V	E	N	T	I	O	N	S	
	V	I	R	T	U	A	L					
			P	L	O	U	G	H				
						T	R	A	C	T	O	R
S	P	A	C	E	X	S	T	A	T	I	O	N

What do you remember?

forecast, remote control, shuttle, exploring, planet, bomb, defuse, modern, operate, Humans, exist, research, spin-off, control, satellite

2 The correct word

1. defuse 2. control 3. research 4. explore 5. spin-off 6. modern 7. forecast 8. humans

What do you remember?

refrigerator, dry, cell phone, switch (it) on, electricity, blackout, high-tech, intelligent

3 Blackout!

blackout, electricity, dry, refrigerator, switch on, cell phone, intelligent, high-tech

4 Definition

1. c, 2. a, 3. b, 4. b, 5. c, 6. a

What do you remember?

washing machine, leak, Remove, sink, plug, flood, electrical, by, tumble drier, cook, run away, cut off, faucet

5 What can you say?

1. b, 2. a, 3. e, 4. c, 5. d

6 Phonetics

1. run away 2. cook 3. cut off 4. electrical 5. washing machine 6. sink 7. leak 8. tumble drier 9. flood

What do you remember?

keep, hairdryer, socket, adaptor, useful, lamp, light bulb, microwave, turn (my cell phone) on, dead, switch, curtain

7 Which word is it?

1. microwave 2. curtains 3. sockets 4. light bulb 5. lamp 6. dead

What do you remember?

code, order, sleep, on time, plus, warning, recording, brushed, stress

8 Jumbled crossword

					1↓					2↓			
					B					P			
					R					L			
					U		4↓			U			
				3→	S	T	R	E	S	S			5↓
					H		E						S
					E		C						L
			7↓		D	6→	O	N	X	T	I	M	E
			O				R						E
			R	8→	C	O	D	E					P
			D				I						
			E				N						
9→	W	A	R	N	I	N	G						

What do you remember?

mountains, factory, workers, illegal, glasses, suspense, secret, on, agent, alien

9 More letters than you need

1. agent 2. workers 3. alien 4. suspense 5. factory 6. mountains

10 Find the mistakes

1. cop, secret 2. to, illegal 3. wear, glasses 4. movie, alien 5. there's, suspense 6. factory, mountains

What do you remember?

across, political, legal, toothache, dentist, flare, pain, couple, band, robbers

11 Word search

Q	U	L	D	C	V	J	S	C	A	A	T	R	S
T	F	E	F	T	E	T	H	H	E	R	A	V	E
O	V	G	L	F	L	A	R	E	K	T	T	E	A
O	B	A	A	R	E	P	T	B	O	A	T	A	B
T	I	L	T	O	I	F	Y	U	R	C	S	E	A
H	N	C	H	B	W	A	E	H	H	R	I	P	N
A	I	A	E	B	L	E	A	F	W	O	S	O	D
C	N	W	W	R	O	B	B	E	R	S	I	L	P
H	S	F	Q	L	I	N	T	E	O	S	I	I	S
E	P	A	A	I	N	K	I	E	U	L	L	T	S
P	A	I	N	E	R	E	R	T	L	O	S	I	Y
C	D	E	N	T	I	S	T	X	Q	U	I	C	I
U	I	B	A	N	R	R	E	E	C	O	O	A	U
P	L	E	G	A	E	E	C	C	O	U	P	L	E
L	A	C	V	R	R	I	S	Y	T	I	U	C	A

What do you remember?

boss, get it, solar system, isn't (pleased with his grade) either, piece, around, agency, spaceship, solar, scare, pass, little

12 What kind of word?

Verb: get it, scare, pass
Adjective: solar, little
Noun: boss, solar system, piece, agency, spaceship
Other: not either, around

What do you remember?

social security number, security, erase, memory, visa, actually, undercover, discovered, bug, hell, social, risk

13 Questions and answers

1. f, 2. d, 3. g, 4. e, 5. c, 6. b, 7. a

What do you remember?

whole, on board, crew, describe, distance, object, V-shaped, air traffic controller, report, thought, simple, investigator

14 Which word is it?

1. whole 2. thought; dentist 3. object 4. air traffic controller 5. simple 6. investigator 7. crew 8. bugs

What do you remember?

cost, Record, IQ, report, fix, apartment, dripping, control, bathtub

15 Questions and answers

1. c, 2. b, 3. f, 4. e, 5. a, 6. d

What do you remember?

cook, as, motel, plug, sink, faucet, exact, choice, task

16 Odd man out

1. bed 2. fun 3. refrigerator 4. exact 5. pacemaker 6. to explore

17 Missing letters

1. as 2. exact 3. choice 4. motel 5. cook 6. task 7. faucet 8. sink 9. plug

What do you remember?

dripping, launch, spaceship, textbook, length, cord, closed, fridge, scientific, mechanic, control, agency

18 Word search

E	P	E	D	R	A	I	M	V	L	E	C	W	O
P	L	P	R	W	T	E	X	T	B	O	O	K	H
S	A	K	Z	L	Y	R	S	T	I	L	N	D	T
C	L	O	S	E	D	H	I	P	E	L	T	B	Y
I	A	B	O	N	Z	O	D	R	G	O	R	P	N
E	U	V	A	G	E	N	C	Y	A	E	O	K	T
N	N	S	R	T	N	S	S	R	P	Y	L	N	O
T	C	A	L	H	E	D	R	I	P	P	I	N	G
I	H	P	U	S	M	R	R	G	L	I	T	C	A
F	R	I	D	G	E	C	G	U	A	V	O	T	M
I	G	F	Y	B	N	M	E	C	H	A	N	I	C
C	O	R	D	R	S	P	A	C	E	S	H	I	P

Revision

→ 1. couple 3. space 5. operate 9. shuttle 10. equipment 13. warning 15. electricity 16. dry 17. toothache 19. robber 22. alien 23. robot

↓ 1. cell phone 2. hairdryer 4. code 6. curtain 7. illegal 8. suspense 9. stress 11. tractor 12. legal 14. light bulb 16. defuse 17. turn on 18. useful 20. bomb 21. agent

Unit 4

What do you remember?

national park, scenery, tribes, reservations, canyon, cowboys, ranch, trucks, highway, sacred

1 My day in my dad's truck

1. truck 2. canyon 3. tribe 4. cowboys 5. highway 6. scenery

What do you remember?

fabulous, casino, trucker, rodeo, Interstate, sight, motorbike, diner, transport, goods

2 The correct word

1. diner 2. Interstate 3. casinos 4. transport 5. fabulous 6. sight 7. motorbike 8. rodeo

What do you remember?

acres, riding, western, square dance, cattle, hill, own, horseback riding, dusty

3 Definition

1. c, 2. a, 3. a, 4. c, 5. b, 6. a

4 The cowboy

We love our ranch! We've got six thousand acres. It's fantastic for horseback riding.

What do you remember?

join, whatever, skill, cattle drive, roping, (park) ranger, deep, take a bus tour, campfire, mule

5 More letters than you need

1. roping 2. campfire 3. deep 4. mule 5. skill 6. whatever

6 Our visit to the ranch

bus tour, acres, roping, cattle drive, whatever, skill, join, cowboys, campfire

What do you remember?

campfire, wood/forest, missed out on, all inclusive, costs, minimum, cabin, wood/forest, No way, camper, underwater, photography, course

7 Jumbled crossword

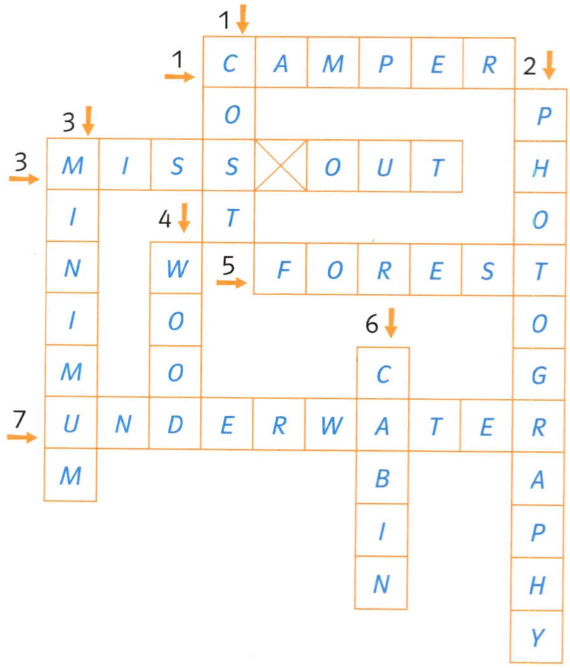

What do you remember?

counselor, mail, offer, rafting, whitewater, tracks, identify, bow, arrows, produces, nature, pros and cons

8 What's the word?

1. to mail 2. track 3. bow and arrow(s) 4. nature 5. to offer 6. pros and cons 7. counselor 8. to produce

What do you remember?

holiday, hotline, dinner, rest area, stranded, delayed, chaos, exit, breakdowns, sunny side up, over easy, By the way, comfortable

9 Odd man out

1. sunny side up 2. stranded 3. delayed 4. arrow 5. pastrami 6. work 7. by the way 8. sacred

What do you remember?

camp, skiing, first of all, Secondly, type, result, cleaner

10 Word grid

											R
	S					S					**E**
	K		T	Y	P	E					S
	I					C					U
F	I	R	S	T		O	F		**A**	L	L
	N					N					T
	G					**D**		C			
					C	L	E	A	N	E	**R**
						Y		M			
								P			

For some American tribes this reservation is a **sacred** place.

What do you remember?

trunk, motorway, roadside, frozen, thaw, serves, vast, overwhelming, gorge, Mom, per cent

11 Rhyming words

1. thaw 2. vast 3. serves 4. trunk

12 What can you say?

1. c, 2. f, 3. d, 4. b, 5. a, 6. e

What do you remember?

set off, cross, go places, end up, till, borders, stuff, might, last, barman, Mexican, driver's license, spray

13 Find the mistakes

1. barman, might 2. borders, driver's license 3. Mexican, sprayed 4. ended up, rest area 5. set off, go places 6. chaos, stuff 7. First of all, barmen 8. secondly, till 9. last, exit 10. crossed, canyon

What do you remember?

feel homesick, Bears, for miles, picker, made friends, Hispanics, Spanish, somehow, attracts, ride, access, raid, all right

14 Letter puzzle

						9.					
1.		S	O	M	E	**H**	O	W			
2.					R	**I**	D	E			
3.		H	O	M	E	**S**	I	C	K		
4.					S	**P**	A	N	I	S	H
5.						**A**	C	C	E	S	S
6.		F	R	I	E	**N**	D	S			
7.	A	L	L		R	**I**	G	H	T		
8.				P	I	**C**	K	E	R		

What do you remember?

restroom, entrance, staff, pretty, experience, get lucky, That was a close one, warned, are (not) allowed, anyway, get it, fiddle, stuck, parking lot

15 Questions and answers

1. f, 2. g, 3. a, 4. e, 5. b, 6. d, 7. c

What do you remember?

platform, mechanic, middle, Nowhere, describe, barking, while, half, discovered

16 Word search

P	C	K	N	N	S	A	E	T	O	I	H
O	Q	N	W	W	T	N	M	S	H	K	A
P	E	D	E	S	C	R	I	B	E	C	L
R	S	T	T	I	W	F	D	A	L	M	F
S	F	M	P	M	Y	W	D	R	M	E	K
O	E	T	O	U	C	S	L	K	I	C	Y
R	N	O	W	H	E	R	E	I	A	H	W
G	N	M	H	B	G	W	K	N	E	A	L
I	A	N	I	O	G	E	S	G	A	N	T
E	I	P	L	A	T	F	O	R	M	I	B
S	O	G	E	H	E	A	E	I	N	C	D
D	I	S	C	O	V	E	R	E	D	T	R

Revision

→ 2. rest area 6. Canyon 8. tribe 10. rodeo 11. fabulous 12. chaos 15. end up 16. for miles 18. license 20. barman 22. all 23. highway 24. type

↓ 1. casinos 2. ranch 3. exit 4. make 5. By 7. national park 9. delayed, 10. result 12. comfortable 13. stuff 14. bear, 17. scenery 19. camp 21. sight

Unit 5

What do you remember?

award, statue, album, R&B, backless, outrageous, evening dress, designer, Latino, low-cut, glamorous, production

1 What can you say?

1. e, 2. a, 3. d, 4. c, 5. b

2 More letters than you need

1. designer 2. statue 3. backless 4. award 5. outrageous 6. album

What do you remember?

ceremony, photographer, country, rock, nickname, present, Picture, reggae, carpet, folk, soul, dancehall, pop

3 The correct word

1. Picture 2. photographer 3. folk 4. rocks 5. nickname 6. dancehall 7. soul 8. carpet

What do you remember?

press, held, trophy, member, attention, records, includes, category

4 Life in a pop group

member, record, includes, category, attention, press, holds, trophy

5 Phonetics

1. include 2. member 3. press 4. trophy 5. attention 6. category

What do you remember?

shutter, setting up, string, motion, stills/still pictures, rise, talkie

6 Letter puzzle

1.				D	E	S	I	G	N	E	R
2.					S	T	A	T	U	E	
3.					R	I	S	E			
4.				T	A	L	K	I	E		
5.					A	L	B	U	M		
6.	S	E	T	X	U	P					
7.			M	O	T	I	O	N			
8.						C	A	R	P	E	T
9.			S	H	U	T	T	E	R		
10.				S	O	U	L				
11.				S	T	R	I	N	G		
12.	B	A	C	K	L	E	S	S			

7 Definition

1. c, 2. b, 3. a, 4. a

What do you remember?

cabinets, publish, receive, complex, score, serious, rocket, attached, western

8 Word grid

1. western 2. serious 3. score 4. rocket 5. complex 6. cabinets 7. attached 8. publish 9. receive
The punk band received an award for the loudest **music**.

What do you remember?

inventor, silent movie, directed, stage, silent, motor, pose, produces, shape

9 Questions and answers

1. b, 2. d, 3. e, 4. a, 5. f, 6. c

10 Phonetics

1. stage 2. direct 3. pose 4. silent 5. motor 6. inventor

What do you remember?

chill out, guitar, freestyle, bling bling, gangster, post, forum, register, matter, chat room, view, dissed, rapper, matter

11 Word search

D	F	T	R	A	B	M	R	O	M	D	R	H
I	P	Y	S	F	R	E	E	S	T	Y	L	E
S	O	D	L	A	U	H	G	T	E	R	Y	I
S	S	O	B	F	C	H	I	L	L	O	U	T
E	T	B	L	R	C	D	S	T	Y	U	R	A
D	E	A	I	W	H	F	T	S	V	I	E	W
W	S	D	N	Q	A	H	E	I	N	M	D	S
G	A	N	G	S	T	E	R	N	R	A	A	R
G	Y	M	B	U	R	X	B	A	A	B	E	F
H	D	R	L	I	O	Y	N	E	P	V	R	O
A	I	E	I	I	O	Y	I	W	P	V	T	R
P	M	V	N	L	M	A	T	T	E	R	G	U
P	S	O	G	U	I	T	A	R	R	E	E	M

What do you remember?

form, check out, offer, suburb, indie, homies, musician, drummer, except, disrespect, e-mail, funk, bass, metal

12 Find the mistakes

1. drummer, suburb 2. check out, funk 3. homie, bass 4. record, offer 5. guitar, metal 6. indie, disrespect 7. e-mailed, except 8. musicians, form

What do you remember?

least, heavy metal, alternative, punk, strictly, is into, independent

13 At the record shop

is into, heavy metal, punk, alternative, strictly, independent, least

What do you remember?

boulevard, limousines, broke, lanes, pop, champagne, shadow, edge, vital signs, unfriendly, ass, chorus, chaperons, vital, pristine

14 Which word is it?

1. shadow 2. limousine 3. lane 4. broke

What do you remember?

have no clue, caviar, sip, support, lifestyle, deserves, reminiscing, rocked, daughter, but, Though, raw, No matter, damn, bank

15 Rhyming words

1. daughter 2. deserves 3. raw 4. bank 5. damn 6. though

16 Odd man out

1. I'm sure 2. to rock 3. to destroy 4. lifestyle

What do you remember?

slang, get back to, battle, heart, beat, phrases, context, synonym, jam, set, battles, entertain, volunteer, give it a go, join

17 Missing letters

1. volunteer 2. get back to 3. battle 4. synonym 5. give it a go 6. beat 7. jam 8. entertain 9. phrases 10. set

What do you remember?

refrain, verses, dream, lyrics, scene, guy, hell, machines, by

18 What's the word?

1. machine 2. refrain 3. lyrics 4. hell 5. (to) dream 6. guy 7. scene 8. verse

Revision

→ 4. set up 5. pristine 7. chorus 11. Latino 13. pop 15. post 17. matter 19. string 20. guitar 21. raw 22. form 24. ass 27. drummer 28. shutter 29. chaperon

↓ 1. present 2. diss 3. rise 6. except 8. bling bling 9. forum 10. support 12. photographer 14. outrageous 16. deserve 18. ceremony 23. homie 25. suburb 26. vital